Seize *the* Moment!

MOSAICA PRESS

Seize *the* Moment!

Finding Meaningfulness
in the Here and Now

RABBI YERED MICHOEL VIDERS

Mosaica Press, Inc.
© 2018 by Mosaica Press
Designed and typeset by Brocha Mirel Strizower

ISBN-10: 1-946351-48-2
ISBN-13: 978-1-946351-48-7

Published by:
Mosaica Press, Inc.
www.mosaicapress.com
info@mosaicapress.com

This *sefer* is dedicated to my parents.
For all of your love.
And for all of your time.
And for teaching me to love time.

25 Tevet 5778

Jared Viders is a Jew with a mission: to inspire other Jews to find beauty in their heritage, to discover the joy of a deep relationship with their Creator, and to uncover the meaning and promise within even the mundane experiences of life. To that end, he has compiled short essays of no more than two to three pages on each *parashah* of the Torah. These essays typically include a vignette coupled with some insightful, often humorous observations, which are then linked to an interpretive point in that week's Torah reading. The themes address such areas as human relationships, gratitude and appreciation, responding to adversity and challenge, learning to live with difficult people (including yourself), forgiveness, empathy, and compassion. Overall, the idea is to take ordinary life in all of its apparent drabness and show how it too can be a source of inspiration and growth. Daily life is a wondrous opportunity, a laboratory for self-discovery and spiritual insight.

This is a wonderful, uplifting, and empowering concept, and Reb Jared executes it with skill and finesse in a way that is accessible for all ages and backgrounds. This work is especially suitable for the Shabbat table. Children will enjoy the stories, and adults as well will recognize the foibles of human nature and the need to at least attempt to transcend them. In an age where we unfortunately often lack the ability to concentrate for long stretches of time, it is important to provide people with Torah insights and values that can be digested in small chunks. This work admirably accomplishes that goal.

May the Ribbono Shel Olom grant the author and his *sefer* much success, and may he merit to produce many other works that will sanctify the Name of Heaven and bring our fellow Jews closer to the Creator.

With much blessing,
Yitzchak A. Breitowitz
Rav, Kehillas Ohr Somayach
Jerusalem, Israel

Rabbi S.F. Zimmerman
Rov of Gateshead

שרגא פייבל הלוי זיממערמאן
אב"ד דק"ק גייטסהעד

אונ' פ' שמש ונאבא ושעלית

My dear friend & colleague R' Yared M Viders
is a Marbitz Torah & Yorei Shomayim with a strong
desire to spread the words of Hashem to the masses.
One of the ways he has done so is by sending out a
weekly communication on the Parsha. It incorporates a
thought from the Parsha with a practical lesson for life.
It has been positively received across the spectrum of
Jewry. Mosaic Press has decided to publish them to further
the words & the lessons of the author

It is my Bracha that this book shall be widely accepted
& appreciated. The author & his family should have good health
peace of mind & simchos & nachas

95 BEWICK ROAD, GATESHEAD, NE8 1RR
TEL: 0191 477 1847   FAX: 0191 477 7688

Table of Contents

Mo'adim

Acknowledgments

One's debts of gratitude are rarely (if ever) paid in full. This is particularly true in my case—on account of the fact that I owe so much to so many. Hashem has sent legions of His most dedicated servants who have generously given me of their precious time, energy, wisdom, care, and concern. Our family has benefitted from their benevolence and largesse to a degree far beyond estimation. With sincere apologies to those whom I may have overlooked, I wish to acknowledge the following:

At the outset, I wish to acknowledge Rabbi Doron Kornbluth and the staff of Mosaica Press for all the orchestration and logistics associated with this *sefer*. Thank you for all of your guidance, assistance, and hard work in helping make this vision into a reality.

A special thanks to my dear friend and mentor Meir Moskovitz, who patiently advised me throughout the drafting and editing process.

To Rabbi Schorr, *shlita*, Rosh Hayeshiva of Ohr Somayach Monsey, for his time, patience, and sage counsel on this project and on virtually every other chapter of my life.

To the "front-liners," who made my initial brushes with Torah so compelling and enriching: Rabbi Bausk (although he insists he played no role whatsoever, I am confident that Hashem feels otherwise), Rabbi Ganz, Rabbi LaBrie, Rabbi Rietti, Rabbi Gould, and the rabbis and mentors of the Moodus program.

The Schachter family for opening their home to me—and with it, the radiance of Shabbos and the *simchah* of Torah-true Judaism.

The families and leadership of the Young Israel of Huntington and

Congregation Chai Odom. May you be rewarded handsomely for your *mesirus nefesh* in bringing Jews closer to Hashem, and for the warmth and generosity with which you do so.

To Rabbi Zaitschek and the extended JEP of Westchester family. May you continue to touch the lives of Jews throughout Westchester and beyond.

To the students who have inspired me with their enthusiasm and quest for truth, knowledge, and spiritual growth. May you know the sweetness and fulfillment of giving over Torah to those who truly seek it.

Rabbi Wiener, Rabbi Mandel, and the *hanhalah* at Ohr Somayach's Center program for providing such an enriching and inspiring entrée into the world of yeshiva. The *chizuk* you imparted has gone much further than I could have imagined.

Rabbi Bertram, for hoping and praying that something would go in. Your unparalleled dedication to your students (me included) is a stellar example of what a *rebbi* can mean to his *talmidim*.

The extended "*mishpachah*" of Ohr Somayach (Monsey)—the Roshei Hayeshiva, Rabbi Braun, the entire *hanhalah*, and scores of *talmidim*. Your *mesirus nefesh* to create—and maintain—a venue for Jews to reclaim their spiritual heritage is truly mind-boggling. This *sefer* would not be possible without your willingness to share the timeless wisdom of Torah with the not-yet-knowledgeable.

The *poskim* whose guidance and availability have routinely resolved doubt and generated immense *simchah* as a result thereof: Dayan Kaufman, Rav Orbach, Rav Schabes, Rav Teitelbaum, and Rav Zimmerman. May Hashem grant you the strength and *binah* to continue to provide such heroic dedication to Am Yisrael and those who seek you.

To Rabbi Ginsberg, Rabbi Kokis, and Rabbi Sher for extending me the priceless opportunity to grow from your *chochmas haTorah* and counsel.

To Rav Moskovitz, *shlita*. There are simply no words that could do justice. The impact you have made on my life is readily apparent virtually every single hour of every single day since you brought me under your wing several decades ago. You have stood by my side through thick and through thin, with patience and dedication. You have provided love and encouragement. You brought me *kanfei Shechinah* with the personification of what it means to be an *eved Hashem*, and you have sustained me there via years and years of sage counsel. May our family and this *sefer* be a source of *nachas* for you and for your remarkable family of *ovdei Hashem*.

To my in-laws, for their continued love and support. May you see much *nachas* from your children and grandchildren.

To Mom and Dad, for every ounce of encouragement and dedication from the instant I entered this world. You are consummate parents, stellar role models, and great friends. May Hashem bless you with *nachas* from Zach and his wonderful family and all your grandchildren.

To my beloved wife. You are the brightest star in my universe. Your *mesirus nefesh* for our family and children is extraordinary. May Hashem bless you with the *kochos* to continue with your *avodas ha'kodesh*. May we see much *nachas* from our children and share in the *simchah* of life together.

To our wonderful children. You give us *nachas* day in and day out. May Hashem infuse your days with true *simchas ha'chaim*. May you know the deep-seated pleasure and fulfillment of serving Hashem and may you appreciate the immense privilege to be counted among Am Yisrael.

To Hashem. Thank you for all of Your love and kindness and patience. For filling the world with reasons to live joyfully and the teachers who have opened my eyes to that joy.

Introduction

Days are scrolls; write in them what you wish to remember.

Duties of the Heart, Gate of Self-Accounting

At the age of ten, I often came across a popular ad that suggested, "The best part of waking up is Folgers in your cup." Three decades later, I feel duty bound to offer an alternative perspective to anyone wishing to listen. With all due respect to coffee and its central role in the continued perpetuation of the human species, this book posits that "the best part of waking up" is the priceless, once-in-a-lifetime opportunity to appreciate being alive and the abundant G-d-given blessings that encompass every facet of our being.

This book does not present questions of life and death—I leave those matters to deeper thinkers with grayer beards. Rather, the chapters that follow deal with questions of life: less life or more life. Specifically, the choice we all possess to live more fully or less fully. To live energized, enthusiastic, and joyful, enamored with the beauty of another day and the lessons to be gleaned therefrom, or to live lethargic, uninspired, and oblivious to the abundant goodness and innate meaningfulness that radiates from every corner of Hashem's universe. Few are those who truly cherish their moments on this planet and relish in the greatest privilege known to mankind—the opportunity to live and to thank Hashem for that opportunity. To live deeply and truly. To fill one's days with purposefulness and one's hours with joyfulness.

The seemingly disparate thoughts and episodes contained in the ensuing chapters share a unifying theme—namely, that a vibrant, meaningful connection to Hashem is readily available to anyone with the sensibility to seek it. More than that, this relationship with the *Borei Olam* is not limited to one's *tefillah* or one's Torah learning or even one's mitzvos; rather, it can (and should) be forged at the breakfast table, strengthened during your carpool, and deepened during the seeming humdrum of everyday life. As Rav Dessler wrote, "The truth is that wherever the person is standing, there is always the opportunity for ascent. That place, wherever it is, is his holy Temple."

The ideas expressed here and the vignettes that (hopefully) bring them home are intended to attune us to the symphony performed day in and day out by every nook and cranny of nature—each bespeaking Divine plan and purpose. Mountains. Seas. Sunrise. Sunset. A world teeming with Divine goodness and blessing. Health. Family. Material means. Accomplishments. All set into motion and sustained by Hashem who, like a loving parent, only seeks the best for His children.

Thus, as the chapters unfold, you will encounter Hashem on the ski slopes, in the book store, at the museum, and on the ball field. This capacity to double-click on the seemingly mundane and to unearth the meaningfulness behind that mundane is the hallmark of a Jew endeavoring to perceive life through Torah lenses. Hence, a glass of water is not only a thirst-quencher, but an opportunity to celebrate "that the universe was created by Your word." A new fruit is much more than a tasty, nutritious snack; it presents an occasion to praise Hashem for "granting us life, sustaining us, and enabling us to reach this occasion." As David HaMelech alluded to in *Tehillim*, the path *ad olam* (lit., "to eternity") begins *me'atah* (lit., "from right now").[1]

Empowered by this outlook, one's days become filled with moments to be seized. These moments are latent with profundity to be internalized. As we learn to identify and be "satisfied" with Hashem's "kindliness" that permeates a seemingly plain old "morning," we will have acquired

---

1   *Tehillim* 121:8.

the priceless capacity "to sing and rejoice throughout our days."[2] We will possess the wherewithal to gain entry to a most esteemed group, i.e., those who can claim to truly "love days."[3]

Meaningfulness will be within reach "at all times and at every moment."[4] We will learn to find Hashem in a pain-free walk, a packed fridge, a luscious peach, and a warm spring breeze. With the world seemingly coming apart at the seams and with so much perceived "gloominess" threatening to mute the sweetness of life, I submit that we need these peaches (and experiences like them) more than ever—we need *all* the goodness of life to register more than ever. The day we exercise the courage and the wherewithal to embrace those moments—to take a proper accounting of all that is good in our lives—is the day we become truly rich.

The Talmud[5] discusses the vast distance between the Heavens and earth. It is my sincere hope that this *sefer* helps bridge that gap ever so slightly, by bringing each of us closer to Hashem, to feel His Presence in our day-to-day lives, to appreciate the blessings therein, and to discover a heightened capacity for true *simchas ha'chayim*.

May we merit to live inspired by the words of David HaMelech in our heart and on our mind that indeed, "This is the day Hashem has made, let us rejoice and be glad with it."[6]

---

2   *Tehillim* 90:14.
3   *Tehillim* 34:13.
4   From *Birkas Hamazon*.
5   *Pesachim* 94.
6   *Tehillim* 118:24.

Parashiyos

Chip Off
the Old Block

O ne of the world's most dazzling artistic accomplishments, Michelangelo's marble sculpture *David*, was unveiled in Florence more than five centuries ago. In the summer of 1995, I visited the Galleria dell'Accademia and was mesmerized by this towering, seventeen-foot marble depiction, so lifelike you expect it to walk off the pedestal and order an espresso.

Notwithstanding this awe-inspiring feat of human creativity and craftsmanship, I confess there were other exhibits that were even more captivating. Specifically, there were a number of "unfinished" statues, works in progress that depicted an eerie blend between crude, coarse, unfinished stone and polished, refined marble. Somehow, the juxtaposition of what "was," i.e., a lifeless chunk of stone, and what "could be," namely, a shockingly lifelike depiction, made an even deeper impression than the *David* itself.

From amid those works at the Galleria emerged one of the inescapable realities of life and our sojourn in this world—the notion that true greatness lies within each and every one of us. Not just ho-hum "humanity" but truly exceptional levels of refinement, virtue, sensibility, and selflessness. We are all, at first glance, like that bland, lifeless gray slab of rock. Yet, if we consistently work on refining our character, on discarding that which is coarse and deep-sixing that which is

7

inconsistent with greatness of character, who knows what towering persona we can discover within? Equipped with timeless tools of the trade of self-perfection—our Torah, its perspectives, our classic works of *mussar*, and access to role models who personify those ideals—let us not underestimate what can be achieved.

Who knows what towering persona lies within, waiting to be unearthed by those willing to chip away and chip away?

> *So G-d created man in His image, in the image of G-d He created him; male and female He created them.*[7]
>
> *And Hashem G-d formed the man of dust from the ground, and He blew into his nostrils the soul of life; and man became a living being.*[8]

This powerful combination—the uncultured coarseness of the dust and the towering, sublime perfection of the soul—a strange *shidduch* indeed, lies at the crux of the human condition. The grace with which we navigate this dissimilar duality lies at the heart of our life's mission.

This notion permeates the Torah's narratives and teachings. Its precepts provide the blueprints to live—indeed thrive—notwithstanding the dilemmas and confusion inherent in the body-soul paradigm. Viewed in this light, even a seemingly dreary, morbid verse (pertaining to the execution of a capital offender, of all people) provides a dose of relevant meaningfulness to those who seek it. In this regard, the Torah states, "You shall surely bury him on that day, for a hanging person is an insult of G-d."[9] Rashi explains, "It is a degradation of the King, for man is made in the likeness of His image."

Far from the echelons of good character and virtue, this depraved individual, who stooped to the abyss of human conduct by committing a capital offense, is nevertheless accorded a modicum of respect and

---

7   *Bereishis* 1:27.
8   Ibid. 2:7.
9   Ibid. 21:23.

decorum. Why? Not because of his lineage or his criminal defense attorneys. Because he, at his core, shares a "likeness of his Maker." Notwithstanding his unseemly demise, a connection and resemblance to the Divine remains intact and inseverable.

We can each lay claim (through no accomplishment of our own) to the privilege of being human. Lest we resign ourselves to menial lives of quiet desperation, let us not neglect the greatness that lies within. As our days and years unfold, let us continue to unearth the diamond—the true mensch—that can be produced with persistent and unflagging efforts to achieve greatness of character.

Noach

Give Me a World

For many children, the highlight of Simchas Torah occurs during the dancing in shul when, at the end of each *hakafah*, those on hand shout out "*Moshe Emes…*" while aging parents launch their youthful kids skyward again and again. (Why they love this repetitive attempt to defy gravity, while wrenching their father's back, I'm not exactly sure—but I suspect the candy-binge has something to do with it.) In any event, one Simchas Torah, I faced a dilemma of epic proportions. On the one hand, I had been given the golden and priceless opportunity to dance with the Sefer Torah during the ensuing *hakafah*. That's good news, right? Well, not necessarily. My four-year-old was slowly putting two and two together: Wait a second, if Daddy's holding the Sefer Torah…well, who in the world is going to launch me during *Moshe Emes*?!

In the nick of time, an acquaintance of mine politely offered, "Maybe your son wouldn't mind if, just this once, I would throw him up? After all, you'll be holding a Torah!" Besides my gratefulness for having been bailed out of a seemingly intractable parental quagmire, I was really quite impressed with this young man's sensibility and perceptiveness. He was a single fellow, probably just north of twenty years old. He didn't really know firsthand what it's like to be a father of a four-year-old. He had been on his feet for several hours and could just as well opt to take a load off. Open a *sefer*. Catch a drink.

No. He was able to assess a situation from *someone else's* vantage point and, as a result, selflessly offer to help enrich the life of another. Was it a *major* act of kindness and self-sacrifice on his part? No. Did it cost much in terms of time or money? No. Would a self-centered person have made the same offer? Most assuredly not.

So Noach went forth, and his sons, his wife, and his sons' wives with him. Every living being...and every bird, everything that moves on earth came out of the Ark...[10]

One has to wonder, why did Noach need to spend an *entire year* on the ark tending to thousands of species of wildlife? Wasn't the ark just a safe haven in which to hide out until the deluge had eliminated the earth's wicked inhabitants? If that be the case, let the generation drown out in forty days' time, bring the ark "back to harbor," and, voilà, start with a new, squeaky-clean world under Noach's sage counsel.

Apparently, the ark was more than just a dry place where Noach and his family could chill out during the flood. Rather, as Rav Moskovitz, *rav* of Boston's Congregation Chai Odom, explains, it was a year-long crash-course immersion in total selflessness—the very *middah* that was necessary in order to properly reestablish the new world on the foundations of kindliness and generosity. Since selfishness and unfettered taking doomed the generation of the Flood (e.g., taking others' wives, taking others' money), that entire taking impulse needed to be uprooted and supplanted with a giving impulse that would permeate every nook of the post-Flood world. In this respect, Noach's tireless, selfless service to the entire animal kingdom was more than just a glorified zookeeper role ensuring the survival of all species. Rather,

> Mankind was rebuilt with the hope that man's coarser taking impulse would be supplanted by man's nobler giving impulse.

---

the entire scenario was orchestrated so that Noach could acquire in spades (and instill in his family) this perspective on life and one's role in the universe.

Against this backdrop, the world at large can be viewed as an expression of *chessed*—not only Hashem's kindliness in giving us a world, but also His expectation that the world endures and prospers on account of man's personal acts of generosity and kindliness.

Lech Lecha

Meet the Teacher

Come Friday morning, all the children in Mrs. Weinberg's first-grade class eagerly look forward to the highlight of the school week: the Shabbos Party. The classroom is transformed into a home that's ready for Shabbos, amid great fanfare and anticipation. The toys and games are neatly put aside while the desks are rearranged for the lavish and festive meal. Smocks are swapped for more elaborate Shabbos clothes. Finally, the makeshift Shabbos table is adorned with warm challahs, a Costco-size bottle of grape juice, and plenty of nosh to keep the natives happy.

To preside over this esteemed event, two students are tapped to play the highly sought-after roles of the Shabbos Tatty and Shabbos Mommy. Today is little Yoni's long-awaited opportunity to star as the Shabbos Tatty. He enthusiastically dons the classroom's (disheveled) Shabbos hat and confidently hoists his silver (plated) goblet to make Kiddush for the class. He pauses. Exhales. Sighs. "What a week it was. I can't get over how the market took such a downturn. We got creamed. Creamed. Absolutely creamed. *Oy veizmir*. OK. What can you do..." He then proceeds to belt out the appropriate blessings, while the class looks askance, wondering what in the world Yoni was talking about.

Despite being a seasoned elementary school teacher (who thought she had seen everything), Mrs. Weinberg is caught off guard by Yoni's remarks. She runs the whole episode past her colleague, Mrs. Goldstein. Upon hearing the story, Mrs. Goldstein comments, "That's so interesting. Today I had a similar event at *our* Shabbos party. Before little Moshe made his Kiddush for the class, he paused, exhaled, smiled, and said, 'And of course, I want to thank Mommy for putting together such a beautiful meal. I am so happy that we are all together for Shabbos,' and then he (similarly) proceeded to belt out the appropriate blessings."

The contrast spoke volumes about the Shabbos atmosphere that permeates the two children's respective homes.

And Abram heard that his brother [Lot] was taken captive, and he led forth his initiates who had been born in his house.[11]

Rashi comments on the word "initiates" (*chanichav*) and explains that the "root of the word *chanichav* stems from that of *chinuch*, i.e., the beginning of the entry of a person…into a craft in which he is destined to stay."

One of the hallmarks of a Jewish home is the emphasis placed upon education. Our bookshelves are lined with volumes containing timeless wisdom. Jews of all ages and stages are perpetually seeking to deepen their understanding of the Torah in any one of dozens of contexts (from macro philosophy to micro halachah). Teachers and educators are (deservedly) held in high esteem, and portraits of legendary Rabbis possessing sterling character grace our walls.

In this universe, where knowledge (not just *what* one knows, but the sincerity with which one *pursues* knowledge) is the coin of the realm, we refer to the education of our children as "*chinuch*." As Rashi explains, the notion of *chinuch* is much broader and more multidimensional than mere literacy or an accumulation of facts and figures. It's about creating, sustaining, and instilling an orientation to life and to Torah "which one is destined" to hold onto for life. It's an all-encompassing

---

11   *Bereishis* 14:14.

outlook. One that an experienced Torah educator described as being "caught, not taught."

Along these lines, Rabbi Rokowsky, my Rosh Yeshiva at Yeshiva Ohr Somayach (Monsey), once offered what he considered to be the single most fundamental benchmark in the approach of parents to *chinuch*. "You should know," he told me, "that children are very attuned—not to what their parents are *actually* doing, but to what their parents' truly *wish* they were doing." When they sense that Daddy *truly* enjoys his time davening in shul, that Mommy is *sincerely* excited about the opportunity to do a *chessed* for someone in need, that the parents' *really* look forward to Shabbos together—it all feeds into an environment of love, positivity, enthusiasm, self-worth, and *simchas ha'chayim*. On the other hand, if Daddy's participation in homework is distracted by the buzzing, vibrating cell phone that he's fidgeting with every three minutes, or if Mommy's morning routine is one unpleasant string of tasks-to-accomplish—get dressed, eat breakfast, pack your lunch, make the bus—then we've done a disservice to our long-term goal of meaningful *chinuch*, i.e., of creating an orientation to life and Torah in which our children will be "destined to stay."

While eulogizing Yitzchak Yaakov Rosenthal, *z"l*, one of his sons-in-law related how the departed repeatedly taught his children (and grandchildren) to know (and rejoice in knowing) that "Hashem is," of all things, "beautiful." Loaded with joie de vivre, he would set the stage by saying, "Hashem is..." and let his listener (be it child or grandchild) finish with a triumphant "beautiful!"

This perspective became so ingrained in his persona that upon coming out of a protracted coma, one family member initiated, "Dad, Hashem is..." and sure enough, Mr. Rosenthal, on the spot, notwithstanding all the hardship, declared, "beautiful!"

Like it or not, we are all educators. Whether we are on the faculty or not. Whether we take attendance or mark papers. Whether or not we have tenure or a special parking spot. We are *all* in *chinuch*. Sometimes we teach young children. Sometimes our students are much to our senior. On some occasions, we teach from a textbook or lesson plan. On other occasions, life is our textbook and we teach by example. Who knows what others may glean from our conduct. In this capacity, life presents no shortage of "teachable moments." May we merit to capitalize on all of them and inspire many "initiates" who will happily and confidently carry the torch of Avraham Avinu's legacy.

Vayeira

Full Esteem Ahead

To tell the truth, most of the phone calls received at our home are looking for someone *other* than me. My kids get calls from friends hoping to set up playdates or seeking confirmation of sundry homework assignments. My wife gets calls from neighbors orchestrating carpool and coordinating *chessed* projects. That basically leaves the telemarketers, political candidates, and fund-raisers who are interested in schmoozing with the (so-called) "head of household."

Anyway, there is one woman who calls (frequently) to speak with my wife. On those occasions when I pick up the phone, she provides a free, easy, and thoughtful gift to my marriage—for instead of simply asking "Is your *wife* available?" she (for as long as I can remember) asks, "Is your *eishes chayil* home?" Now, was that such a big deal? Does it cost her any time or any money? Absolutely not. Just an ounce of thoughtfulness and a willingness to remind me how special, enthusiastic, dedicated, and praiseworthy my wife *really* is. It costs her nothing. To the listener, though, it is priceless.

Who wouldn't want (indeed, cherish) such an advocate and public relations campaign? Imagine someone meets my wife in the grocery store and says, "Viders? That name is so familiar. Wait...does your husband have a reddish-grayish beard? I heard him speak once and he has the greatest sense of humor. We were rolling in the aisles. And we were all *so* inspired from his words!"

Now, such a vignette isn't very likely to happen (perhaps *totally* beyond the realm of credibility). But if it did, wouldn't it make my wife feel like a million bucks?! Wouldn't she think to herself, "Yeah. She's right, my husband is a funny, inspiring kind of guy." Wouldn't I feel grateful to that woman for reminding my wife what a terrific sense of humor I have?! It's a total win-win. Just a few words that will invariably generate a heightened sense of satisfaction, happiness, and appreciativeness.

> *They said to [Avraham], "Where is Sarah your wife? And he said, "Behold—in the tent!"[12]*
>
> Rashi: *"The angels knew where Sarah was but they nonetheless asked to make it known that she was modest in order to endear her to her husband."*

From all indications, one can reasonably postulate that Avraham and Sarah shared a wonderful and enriching marriage, buoyed by a substantial degree of mutual respect and esteem. So far as we know, she was the most righteous woman on the planet (perhaps ever) and Avraham's unswerving partner in his mission of bringing truth, loving-kindness, and knowledge of Hashem to the world. They had successfully navigated many decades of matrimonial harmony—notwithstanding many personal hardships, traumatic events, and upheaval. They graduated the *shalom bayis* school of hard knocks with flying colors. Indeed, they will remain the model Jewish home for eternity. Do the angels *really* need to "endear her to her husband" any further?

The lesson here is that we can, with relative ease, take on a new mission in life—i.e., to raise people's esteem in the eyes of those whom they love. A teacher tells a parent what a delight it is to have her daughter in class. A parent mentions to a teacher how her child loves the

---

12   *Bereishis* 18:9.

stories her *morah* gives over. A shopkeeper mentions to a husband that his wife has such a pleasant disposition (and not just because she's a liberal spender!). A guest mentions to his host, "I've heard your wife's potato kugel is out of this world." The permutations are endless. And the payoff—in terms of bolstering relationships, ratcheting up endearment, enhancing one's sense of self-worth—is inestimable.

Opportunities abound to deepen others' appreciation for the people in their life.

Needless to say, I am not advocating untruths, hyperbole, or flattery. If a person has two left thumbs, there is little to be gained in suggesting that he's Mr. Fix-It around the house. If your spouse has never managed to attend a *simchah* on time, what's the point of praising her "you can set your watch to it" punctuality? The point is merely this—for the wise-hearted individual with a discerning eye and a sincere desire to elevate someone's esteem in the eyes of others, opportunities abound.

Along similar lines, one should not easily shirk opportunities to praise others directly (least of all his or her spouse). As the legendary Rebbetzin Kanievsky advised, "The words a wife uses to praise her husband are *the most precious words she will say in her life*. There is never a situation where one spouse gives another too much praise."

We are well aware of the destructive impact that negative, critical speech can wreak on relationships (and among spouses). However, it's simply not enough to merely *avoid* uttering such negative sentiments. The capacity to speak is what sets us apart as human beings. The capacity to speak positively—in such a way that we routinely (and creatively) lift the spirits and esteem of those around us—is the hallmark of nobility that we must strive for.

Chayei Sarah

Pitcher Perfect

Years ago, an entrepreneur posed the following question to Klal Yisrael's most eminent halachic authority, none other than Rav Yosef Shalom Elyashiv, *zt"l*. Seems business required that this gentleman travel from New York to Australia. When booking his flight, the travel agent posed two possible options: the first was a straight shot from JFK to Sydney, but would require him to traverse the International Date Line, whereby he would "miss" a *Shacharis*. (Without getting into the nitty-gritty, suffice to say that the calendar day would essentially pass from today to tomorrow without twenty-four hours elapsing in between.) This option was both more direct and less costly.

Alternatively, he could fly via Los Angeles and essentially circumnavigate the globe in the opposite direction. While both more expensive (on account of additional fuel costs) and less efficient (a twenty-two-hour ordeal), this second option essentially sidestepped the halachic quagmire associated with the International Date Line and would afford him an opportunity to daven all the proper *tefillos* at all the proper times.

What Rav Elyashiv ultimately decided, I know not. What this globe-trotting voyager ultimately opted for, I have no clue. (I presume the travel agent advocated for the greater fee). Rav Elyashiv's response, however, offers a priceless, piercing observation into the way we approach our *avodah*. "But the *tefillah* that you would miss—how do you know," asked the venerable Rav, "if that particular *tefillah* is not the one that would be answered favorably and bring the *yeshuos* you are seeking?"

One afternoon, I arrived to give a class, only to find out that—well, how shall we put it—there were *plenty* of good seats still available. The sparse attendance, I confess, may have tempered my enthusiasm and who knows if I truly brought my A-game to the classroom that day. One call to Yerushalayim, however, would effectively recalibrate my approach to such a situation. When I recounted what had transpired, one of my *rebbeim* (in his inimitable style) fired back, "Do you know what will become of those students that attended? How do *you* know which student is going to be the next *marbitz Torah*? How do *you* know which guy is going to emerge as a supporter of Torah? You have to deliver your best because you never know which student is going to go on and accomplish for the Jewish People."

The servant [Eliezer] ran toward her and said, "Let me sip, please a little water from your pitcher." She said, "Drink, my lord," and she hurried and she lowered her pitcher to her hand and gave him drink. When she finished giving him drink, she said, "I will draw water even for your camels, until they have finished drinking." So she hurried and she emptied her pitcher into the trough and kept running to the well to draw water; and she drew for all his camels.[13]

Eliezer was privy to a singular display of Rivkah's kindliness, selflessness, and sensibility. On the basis of that singular outpouring of *chessed*

---

13   *Bereishis* 24:17–20.

toward him, his entourage, and his camels, Eliezer proceeded to offer Rivkah an opportunity for eternity—to become one of the matriarchs of the Jewish Nation. To take her place alongside Sarah as a Mother of Am Yisrael. To ascend as both the torchbearer and paradigm of the quintessential Jewish home.

For centuries to come, Jewish parents all over the world will beseech Hashem that their daughters walk in the ways of "Sarah, *Rivkah*, Rachel, and Leah."

For centuries to come, Jews will pour out their hearts in prayer beside her *kever* alongside the progenitors of our nation at Me'aras HaMachpeilah in Chevron.

For centuries to come, Bais Yaakov classes and elementary schools will be packed with students called Rivkah, aspiring to live up to their namesake.

At the risk of sounding cynical (or even heretical), I wonder, did Rivkah harbor second thoughts that day, perhaps wondering what in the world this foreigner was thinking?

Did she waiver at all before volunteering to hydrate the entire pack of dromedaries as well? Maybe let Mr. Stranger discharge the rest of the water-boy duties!

The answers to these questions, quite frankly, are wholly immaterial. Rivkah seized an opportunity to help a forlorn fellow quench his thirst and followed through (with great alacrity) in seeing that his crew and animals were attended to as well. Did she *know* the eternal reward that was awaiting her as a result of this conduct? Absolutely not. Will the shockwaves of her willingness to go above and beyond the call of duty ripple for eternity? For sure.

> When going the extra mile seems unwarranted, don't squelch your inner voice cheering you on beyond complacency.

Hardly a day passes without an opportunity to truly enhance someone else's well-being. Physically. Emotionally. Mentally. Spiritually. [Helping people's camels is less common.] When going the extra mile seems unwarranted and just "getting by" seems entirely reasonable, don't squelch that inner voice cheering you on beyond complacency. For who knows what greatness of character and eternal reward awaits you.

Toldos

Two Roads

A *baal teshuvah* once chose to attend the nominally Jewish, albeit secular, wedding of a family friend's daughter. It was one of those affairs where the invite had been a matter of course, a gesture of etiquette, but one which easily could have been declined without diminishing the parties' relationship at all. Nevertheless, this young man RSVP'd on the basis of some "sixth sense" that his presence would somehow, someway, change the life of one of the event's attendees. Perhaps one guest would share some deep, perplexing question about the meaning of life and he would be the one to respond with the voice of truth. Perhaps the person sitting next to him would be contemplating marrying a non-Jew and he would be the one to deter them, thereby helping to perpetuate a Jewish lineage for future generations.

Alas, the night came and went without any incident whatsoever. No shining moments of "outreach." No unexpected encounters with anyone looking to ponder the profundities of life and the purposefulness of existence. Later, however, upon introspection, this fellow realized that he had indeed acquired something of immense value that night: a heightened appreciation for the opportunity to lead the life he *himself* had chosen as an observant Jew.

Seemingly, the opportunity to perceive firsthand the way his non-observant life would likely have unfolded provided a poignant and penetrating glimpse into the richness of what he opted for instead. His intuition proved correct. The night made a deep impression on—of all people—himself.

This young, secular Jewish bride and groom for sure possessed plenty of praiseworthy values—they were (probably) generous and kind; they (appeared to be) happy and carefree; they (presumably) would hold down positive, productive jobs; would have 2.2 kids and a Labrador; would give to the Lung Society; and would (ideally) aspire to make the world a better place. Was there anything so wrong with that? No. Not really…

And yet, for the one who opted to reconnect with his authentic, Torah-based roots, to live the Yiddishkeit of his ancestors, there was indeed an infinitely richer and more purposeful existence in store. One infused with the radiance of Shabbos and the Jewish holidays. One refined by the classic works of *mussar* and character improvement. One enriched with the timeless wisdom of Tanach and the Talmud. One empowered by a career of davening. One buoyed with *emunah* and *bitachon*. And one inspired to excel in *avodas Hashem* as a lifelong expression of gratitude for the trillions of undeserved kindnesses He bestows upon us and our planet day in, day out. A life brimming with spirituality, purposefulness, and fulfillment. This realization alone was priceless and, indeed, well worth the trip…

As a good Jew from Brooklyn once taught me, it is no coincidence that Yaakov and Eisav were born as twins. In this respect, they represent the closest carbon copy we could imagine—same father, same mother, same gene pool, born under the same *mazal*, raised in the same household, probably rode the same bicycles and played on the same Little League team. Amid this nearly identical upbringing, one blazes an illustrious path of righteousness and becomes the torchbearer for Am Yisrael, while the other gets entangled with unsavory pursuits that ultimately spell his spiritual downfall and dizzying disappointment.

Their respective paths in life—and the paths *we* choose—often remind me of the ramp from Route 17W onto the New York State Thruway.

At that juncture, the "path" to Buffalo veers off from the "path" to Manhattan by a mere few feet. Six and a half hours (and almost 370 miles) later, you'll realize that veering North as opposed to South has created a staggering differ-ence in location.

Appreciate the good fortune to have chosen the road less traveled...the road of *emes* and eternity.

So it is in our lives. We, too, possess the op-portunity to choose growth, to choose greatness, and to choose eternity. As Robert Frost put it:

> *Two roads diverged in a yellow wood,*
> *And sorry I could not travel both...*
> *I shall be telling this with a sigh*
> *Somewhere ages and ages hence:*
> *Two roads diverged in a wood, and I—*
> *I took the one less traveled by,*
> *And that has made all the difference.*

Choose wisely, for so, so much hangs in the balance. To the extent we have done so already, we must live with the deep-seated appreciation that Hashem has helped us and guided us "and separated us from those who go astray, gave us the Torah of truth, and implanted within us eternal life."[14]

---

14   From the prayer of *"Uva L'Tzion."*

Vayeitzei

Double Vision

These twenty years I [Yaakov] have been with you [Lavan]…That [animal] which was mangled I never brought you—I would bear the loss from my hand…This is how I was: By day, heat consumed me, and snow by night; my sleep drifted from my eyes. This is for me twenty years in your household…and you changed my wage ten times…[15]

After Yaakov's emboldened defense of his unflinching loyalty throughout his tenure shepherding Lavan's flocks, Lavan responds incredulously, "The daughters are my daughters, the children are my children, and the flock is my flock, and all that you see is mine."[16]

Uh…hello? Ground control to Lavan. That's *all* you have to say in response to Yaakov's declaration?! What have you to say regarding Yaakov's heroic commitment to your welfare? Have you no recognition whatsoever for his efforts? Have you no appreciation for his toil?

---

15   *Bereishis* 31:38–42.
16   Ibid. 31:43.

Does this sound familiar? Your life is whirring at such a pitch that you're just barely managing to keep some semblance of order to the chaos. You've just got home and are either: (1) gearing up for the escapades associated with homework, "bedtime, bath time, and beyond time" with the kids; or (2) winding down for a quiet supper and a good book [depending on what stage of life you're in] when...all of a sudden, some telemarketer from Wyoming with an (almost) intelligible command of English is on the line wondering "if now is a good time to speak?" Well...to be honest, "NO! It's an incredibly inconvenient time for you even to think about calling me (unsolicited, no less!). One and a half kids are in the bath. One is swinging on the chandelier and another has a report due tomorrow on some explorer who discovered Panama."

Where's the disconnect here? Simply put, I've come to view the world as consisting of two types of people: those who understand my life and those who don't. The people who call in the middle of dinnertime usually just don't get it. I can't even blame them. The client who calls at seven thirty at night to discuss his particular matter. He just doesn't get it. He envisions I have nothing better to do with my life than to sit patiently and await his call. And those local chimney sweepers who call me every year (incessantly)—they *surely* don't get it. I don't even own a chimney.

Successful interactions with others invariably call upon us to assess how things look from "their" perspective. Even if someone else's assessments or expectations are ridiculously way out of whack, the more we can appreciate where *they* are coming from, the better we'll be able to dialogue effectively and problem-solve and/or strategize (as necessary). Disconnect between people is often the by-product of the parties' inability to truly grasp how the other is sizing up a particular situation.

Connectedness hinges largely on our ability to assess life from someone else's vantage point.

As we encounter the various personalities in our life, we can spare ourselves frustration and hassle by acknowledging that often, other people we interact with aren't trying to be difficult—rather, their perception of our situation is simply way off base. Whatever the case may be, just accepting that fact (rather than attempting to change it) may ultimately be more fruitful in the long run.

Vayishlach

Brothers-in-Arms

Nearly fifty years ago, a British pop group launched a song entitled, "He Ain't Heavy, He's My Brother." This very notion is one that Jews have held sacrosanct from their very inception, dating back to Avraham Avinu and his uncompromised dedication to his wayward nephew Lot. Since then, the hallmark of the Jewish people has remained their unspoken yet tangible camaraderie for one another. Indeed, our history is laden with legendary tales of self-sacrifice and selflessness...not to mention the thousands of untold stories that play themselves out week in and week out in Jewish communities the world over.

Our family received a truly inspiring book entitled, *Emunah with Love and Chicken Soup*, which will surely warm one up on a cold wintry night. Sara Yoheved Rigler's five hundred-page tribute to the late Rebbetzin Henny Machlis captures the spirit of this Brooklyn native's extreme degree of dedication to the well-being of every Jew—every human, really—who merited to know her and her illustrious family. Each Shabbos, as the book enumerates, the family hosted well over one hundred guests from every walk and stripe in their less-than-lavish, cramped Yerushalayim apartment. Not just the interesting personalities that are a pleasure to host, but many, many undesirable guests who had nowhere else to call home and no one else to call family.

One guest by the name of Oren suffered from a mental illness that rendered him a volatile and unpredictable persona (at best). Nevertheless, "Henny always treated Oren with endless patience and love... She had a lot of things going on in her life, but Oren could be here for hours talking to her, and she always made him feel important and loved. *Not all people need food, but all people need love*—love and attention and someone to listen to them..." [emphasis added].[17]

Not all people need food, but everyone needs love.

And it came to pass on the third day, when they were in pain, that two of Jacob's sons, Shimon and Levi, Dinah's brothers, each took his sword and they came upon the city...[18]

At this point in the *Chumash*, aren't we well-versed with Yaakov's family tree? Of course Shimon and Levi are Dinah's brothers. They share the same father. It's not like they're second cousins-in-law, three times removed. Anticipating this question, Rashi explains, "Because they risked themselves for her, they are referred to as 'her brothers.'"

True brotherhood—in the Torah sense of the word—goes beyond biological realities and shared upbringings. It is an emotional and psychological kinship that is honed through one's thoughtfulness and actions on behalf of one's fellow Yidden. That is the ultimate emblem of true depth of character, and something for each of us to strive for. For "not all people need food, but all people need love—love and attention and someone to listen to them."

---

17   Sara Yocheved Rigler, *Emunah with Love and Chicken Soup* (Shaar Press, 2016), p. 73.

18   *Bereishis* 34:25.

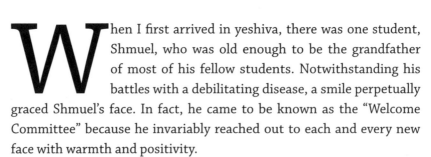

Vayeishev

More Than Meets the "I"

When I first arrived in yeshiva, there was one student, Shmuel, who was old enough to be the grandfather of most of his fellow students. Notwithstanding his battles with a debilitating disease, a smile perpetually graced Shmuel's face. In fact, he came to be known as the "Welcome Committee" because he invariably reached out to each and every new face with warmth and positivity.

More than just a mere "*Shalom aleichem*," Reb Shmuel would proceed to introduce any newcomers to all the other classmates (and the teacher)—and would add his simple, understated, signature line, "He's wonderful." "This is Aaron. He's wonderful." "This is Dovid. He's wonderful." "Oh, and this is our rabbi—he's really wonderful."

Approximately ten years later, the yeshiva and wider community mourned the loss of Reb Shmuel and his uncanny capacity to recognize that yes, people—with all our foibles and all our imperfections—are truly wonderful. During the shivah period, friends recalled, among others, two sterling aspects of Shmuel's character:

1. His capacity to recognize the good in others (and to give expression to that goodness)
2. His deep-seated humility

One visitor proceeded to explain (with the following vignette) that these two *middos* are really rooted in the same mindset.

> *One of the pious, it is told, passed by the carcass of a dog which gave forth a dreadful odor. His disciples said to him, "How dreadfully does this carcass smell!" He said to them, "How white are its teeth!" They then regretted the disparaging remark they had made about it.*

Nice, meaty (sorry, bad pun) episode with myriad lessons to be gleaned therefrom—the ability to focus on the positive, the notion that different people can absorb vastly different messages from the same encounter, and so on. What always bothered me with this vignette, however, is not *why* the author of the *Chovos HaLevavos* chose to include it in his classic *sefer*, but rather *where* he chose to incorporate it: in his chapter on *humility*. What, exactly, do these lines teach me about being humble?

When this question was posed to Rabbi Chaim Bausk, Rabbi of Young Israel of East Northport, he offered a terrific explanation that offers broad applicability to our lives—far more frequently than our (hopefully) rare encounters with road kill.

Returning to the dog's carcass, what enabled the disciples' teacher to zero in on the whiteness of the teeth was not *only* a by-product of his glass-half-full, focus-on-the-positive, see-the-silver-lining mindset. Rather, the between-the-lines take-home lesson was the fact that the teacher *also* smelled the dreadful odor emanating from the carcass. He wasn't olfactory-challenged. He didn't have a stuffed nose. So why didn't the unsavory aroma torpedo *his* capacity to perceive positivity?

Precisely, explained Rabbi Bausk, because the teacher was so humble of spirit. His humility enabled him to endure *personal* discomfort (on account of the unpleasant smell) while limiting its scope. What was unpleasant to him did not spill over to a degree that it would warp his core desire to be positive and see positive.

> Humility can protect one's perceptiveness from being hijacked by personal discomfort.

In short, humility protected his consciousness from being hijacked by his personal discomfort.

We are, by nature, hard-wired to think first and foremost about ourselves—Am I tired? Am I hungry? How much coffee do I need to get this day underway? Do I feel underappreciated or overwhelmed? And only *then*—after I am "good to go"—am I capable of processing the world at large, that lies beyond me. Hashem's kindnesses. The sunshine. The breeze. The other people in my life and their particular attributes (to praise) or lacks (to strive to fulfill).

This being the case, the more humble a person is, the less self-consumed they are likely to be, and, hence, it will be that much easier for them to see beyond their own immediate needs and agenda.

Yosef HaTzaddik repeatedly exhibits this strength of character—the wherewithal to see beyond his own personal crises. For instance, the Torah informs us that the Yishmaelim's camels "were bearing spices"[19] instead of their usual cargo, i.e., the malodorous petroleum and resin. Rashi elaborates that the Torah is not interested in teaching us the export/import habits of ancient desert-dwellers, but rather to inform us that Hashem went "out of His way" (so to speak) to ensure that Yosef's descent to Egypt would not be *further* exacerbated by an unpleasant smell.

Would such a minor detail register with us? Imagine you're being carted off to prison for a crime you didn't commit. Life as you know it is coming to a crashing halt. All your dreams have gone up in smoke. You may never see your family again and...*wait, what's on the patrol car's radio, is that Vivaldi's Four Seasons I hear?! Oh I just love that score...come to think of it, this nightmare isn't all that bad...* Ridiculous.

Later, when sitting in prison (for yet another crime he didn't commit), Yosef has the emotional equilibrium to perceive on his fellow

---

19   *Bereishis* 37:25.

inmates' faces that "they were aggrieved"[20] *and* had the psychological wherewithal to inquire, "Why are your faces downcast today?" Had Yosef truly been wallowing in his own self-pity, consumed with negative thoughts of "woe is me," and consumed with regret, anger, and anxiety, there's simply no way he would have the emotional bandwidth to make a sincere inquiry into someone else's hardships—or even to notice them at all.

The "I" and the "self" seemingly loom larger than ever. We are no longer hungry, we are "starving" and "famished." The weather is no longer merely hot or cold but rather "sweltering" or "frigid." Situations that were once "frustrating" are now "unbearable." And no one is merely tired anymore, rather we are all "exhausted." Our lacks (and our perception thereof) seemingly far outpace all that is truly going right in our lives. Torah-true humility enables us to transcend our own innate self-awareness. In so doing, humility allows us to tap into the beautiful world that surrounds us and to behold the true sweetness of life.

> We are no longer hungry; we are starving and famished.

---

20   Ibid. 40:6.

Mikeitz

Light through the Night

O n April 18, 1775, American Revolutionary War hero Paul Revere ventured forth on his legendary "Ride" that was later memorialized by poet Henry Wadsworth Longfellow:

Listen, my children, and you shall hear

Of the midnight ride of Paul Revere...

He said to his friend, "If the British march

By land or sea from the town to-night,

Hang a lantern aloft in the belfry arch

Of the North...tower, as a signal light,

One, if by land, and two if by sea;

And I on the opposite shore will be,

Ready to ride and spread the alarm

Through every...village and farm,

For the country-folk to be up and to arm.

Far beyond mere sources of heat or illumination, candles serve as orators. Birthday candles speak, and yet they convey a message entirely different than the candles that accompany one's anniversary dinner.

Stepping into the realm of the spirit, Yarhtzeit candles bespeak words of consolation and remembrance, while the Shabbos candles bespeak *menuchah*. The same oil. The same wick. The same flame—yet each offers a distinctly different connotation and significance to the eye of the beholder.

On my street, the Chanukah lights shine beautifully and elegantly through our neighbors' windows. Down the block there is a residence bearing more lights than the runways at JFK. He's got reindeers and trees and stars and more reindeers. One can only fathom the kilowatt hours that accrue to his utility bill this time of year. I wonder how he sleeps at night amid the glare from his front yard.

And yet we Yidden, all across the globe, gain so much inspiration and *chizuk* from these timeless, simple, plain, and *pashut* lights. The same lights that Yidden have been inspired by for so many centuries. The same lights that have dispelled so much darkness—national and personal—for so many generations.

Chanukah was the last "holiday" implemented by our Sages and thus it is not unreasonable (at all) to conjecture that every message that Am Yisrael would need to span the centuries can be found amid the seemingly soft-spoken *neiros* of Chanukah. So simple and yet so profound. So delicate that a faint breeze could extinguish them and yet so eternal that the winds of change could never snuff them out. For those who wish to see what lies therein, they will surely find meaningfulness, inspiration, and hope.

The winds of change and exile could never snuff out the meaningfulness of the Chanukah lights.

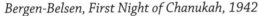

Vayigash

Against the Dying of the Light

Bergen-Belsen, First Night of Chanukah, 1942

I n a true testament to the undying Jewish spirit, a group of weary and grief-ridden Jews gathered in Bergen-Belsen's Barrack 10 to fulfill the mitzvah of lighting the *ner Chanukah*. Rabbi Yisrael Spira, better known as the Bluzhever Rebbe, was tapped to kindle the most humble of menorahs (fashioned out of a raw potato) amid the most harrowing of circumstances.

The Bluzhever chanted the first blessing over the mitzvah and the second blessing commemorating the miracles that Hashem has performed for our nation. Before making the third blessing, *She'hechiyanu*—in which we thank Hashem for having "kept us alive, preserved us, and enabled us to reach this time"—the Rebbe paused, looked behind him, looked back at the *ner*, and then somehow mustered the inner fortitude to utter those powerful words. This, despite the fact that he had recently lost his wife, daughter, son-in-law, and only grandchild.

As recorded in Yaffa Eliach's *Hasidic Tales of the Holocaust*, the assembled inmates joined him in a chorus of weeping, for all of them had also lost their own families. In low voices, choked by irrepressible sobs, they struggled to chant *Maoz Tzur*, which proclaims our steadfast faith in Hashem, no matter how bleak the situation.

Shortly thereafter, Mikel, an irreligious former Bund leader inquired, "Rabbi...you have lit the candles and said, *L'hadlik Ner* and *She'asah Nissim*. Fine and good. Painful as it is to me, I can understand. But what justification do you have in saying *She'hechiyanu*? How can you bless a G-d who has 'kept us alive and preserved us and enabled us to reach this time,' when all around us, thousands of us are dying before our very eyes?"

Casting aside dogma, philosophy, and indignation, the Rebbe conceded softly: "I, too, ask myself this question." Indeed, that is why he had hesitated before reciting that third blessing. "I looked for an answer and finally found one. For I saw that a large crowd had gathered—risking their own lives in so doing—to watch the lighting of the candles. By the very fact that G-d has such loyal Jews—prepared to give their lives for the lighting of the candles, I said to myself, 'This is a special People. To behold such a special People, is, by that very fact alone, reason to recite *She'hechiyanu*.'"

> *And He said, "I am the G-d—G-d of your father. Do not be afraid of descending to Egypt, for I shall establish you as a great nation there."*[21]

While the Torah portrays the descent of Yaakov's family to Mitzrayim as the triumphant, long-awaited reunion with Yosef, anyone who's ever sat through the Pesach Seder knows that this *also* marks the onset of one of the most dreadful eras of our nation's history—the Egyptian exile. Servitude. Genocide. Two hundred ten years of suffering.

And yet, Hashem had promised Yaakov that precisely *"there"* would Hashem establish His People—*our* people—as a great nation. Not

---

21   *Bereishis* 46:3.

playing shuffle-board in Boca Raton. Not sipping lemonade in the Hamptons. Not enjoying a cappuccino at Starbucks. Quite the opposite.

The greatness, majesty, and unflinching loyalty of the Jewish People emerged *precisely* from the shadows of exile.

Our forefathers' travails in Egypt are, ultimately, what minted Klal Yisrael and forged our unbreakable bond with Hashem.

Therein lies one of the keys to the improbable and inexplicable survival of the Jewish Nation. The unique capacity to withstand and endure suffering and exile without forsaking our lifeline to that which is Divine and Eternal. This has been the hallmark of the Jew-in-exile for time immemorial.

The greatness, majesty, and unflinching loyalty of Am Yisrael emerges *precisely* from amid the shadows of (seeming) hopelessness. Be it the threat of extermination at the hands of Haman. Be it the threat of assimilation at the hands of Antiochus (or the present day). Be it the dehumanization at the hands of the Nazis, the Jew is never disconnected from our Source of life. A Jew remains steadfast in our faith, a rose among the thorns.

Vayechi

Mission: Possible

Ever get the feeling that you are in just a *tad* over your head? Several summers ago, on a sweltering July afternoon, our family and countless pieces of luggage were packed into an airport shuttle en route to JFK, where we were slated to fly to Eretz Yisrael in celebration of my fortieth birthday. Lo and behold, as our driver careened around the entry ramp to the George Washington Bridge, the van came to a sudden halt. The van was dead. Hmmm…this "detour" was neither scenic nor part of our itinerary.

While the driver radioed in for help, explaining that "we need a jump," multigenerational pandemonium was slowly unfolding. The stalled van was stationed in a location begging for a collision. The now non-air-conditioned car was quickly becoming unbearable for the younger ones. The older ones, well, they looked somewhat panic-stricken, wondering if we really "need to jump." [They weren't familiar with the notion of "jumping" a car and thus interpreted the driver's jargon as a call for us to "jump" off the bridge.] My wife gave me that look. You know, that look that says, "You've got a plan, right?" While I tried to exude confidence, I was internally in Mayday mode, secretly hoping "my mommy would somehow make this all better!"

Without any other alternative in sight, we offered a *tefillah* to Hashem, and I made my way from the ramp toward toll booth security.

A few moments later, a fully functional fifteen-person, air-conditioned airport shuttle pulled over in front of our motley crew and asked if we were OK and if we could use a lift. Sent via the Divine Dispatcher, Levi the Shuttle Driver *just happened to be* returning from the Catskills en route to Queens and was oh-so-happy to offer us a lift to JFK. In a total state of disbelief, we alighted all the kids and our fifty-two pieces of luggage and were on our way. Thankfully, this van was able to complete the journey to our destination, and we arrived safely at our gate in plenty of time for boarding. Well…that was easy.

Among the many take-home lessons from this less-than-routine trip to the airport was the notion that Hashem possesses an endless number of exit strategies out of an endless number of predicaments. Had I reassured my wife, "Let's just be calm. Hang out for a bit. Probably someone with an empty van en route to Queens will stop off and offer us a ride to the airport. Can you pass me some popcorn?" I probably would have failed miserably in the proactive-resourceful-husband department. That "proposed" solution was simply out of the question and way beyond the boundary of reasonable possibility.

[Yaakov] said to Yosef, "I did not imagine seeing your face, and here G-d has shown me even your offspring!"

Rashi: "It did not enter my mind (lit., my heart did not fill me) to consider the thought that I would see your face again."[22]

> Our *avodah* is to never lose hopefulness, for Hashem has countless exit strategies at His disposal.

Life presents scenario after scenario and, as we navigate those scenarios, we envision an array of outcomes. Some end results are predictable. Others anticipated. Some are remote and others downright incredible.

---

22   *Bereishis* 48:11.

As Jews, the privilege of 24-7 access to the Infinite essentially renders the "impossible" obsolete. Indeed, the very notion should seemingly be erased from our emotional dictionaries and our mindset. There is no relationship that cannot be salvaged. There is no bill that cannot get paid. There is no applicant that cannot find employment. There is no soul that cannot find their *bashert*. And yes, that intermarriage-in-the-making that seems like a fait accompli can, in a heartbeat, be un-accompli'd. Hashem can find a way. He's that Good and that Resourceful and that Creative. He holds all the keys, all the cards, and has no shortage of exit strategies at His disposal.

In a similar vein, upon hearing devastating news about the prognosis of a loved one's health, an observant Jewish family inquired of their physician, "How long does he have to live?" To which the doctor responded, "With you people, you never know."

Be it our long-standing national exile or a personal predicament, our *avodah* is to never lose hopefulness. When Hashem is in the equation, there is simply no such thing as a mission impossible.

Shemos

Worth the Wait

His sister [Miriam] stationed herself at a distance to know what would be done with him [Moshe.][23]

The older sister watched and waited to see what would become of her baby brother's treacherous journey down the Nile. What's the big deal? Wouldn't you do the same? Why does the Torah bother to include this seemingly irrelevant detail in its depiction of Moshe's improbable survival?

Taking it one step further, the Talmud[24] extols Miriam's "waiting" and anticipation as an instance of Divine measure-for-measure. For on account of Miriam's patience at the Nile, all of Klal Yisrael would, generations later, "wait" for Miriam before resuming their odyssey through the Wilderness. Again, the question is readily apparent, what is *so* significant about Miriam's seemingly insignificant decision to "wait" to see what would befall her baby brother?

---

23   *Shemos* 2:4.
24   *Sotah* 12b–13a.

Waiting has never been fun. Today it ranks even higher on our list of frustrations. As the pace of life whirls on at an increasingly dizzying speed, the notion of waiting (for anything or anyone) becomes increasingly exasperating. There's simply *way* too much for us to get done for us to flitter away our precious time with "waiting."

Dr. Seuss, the famous author of dozens of children's books, once described "The Waiting Place" as "a most useless place...for people just waiting. Waiting for a train to go or a bus to come, or a plane to go or the mail to come, or the rain to go or the phone to ring, or the snow to snow or the waiting around for a Yes or No...Everyone is just waiting."

This sentiment has been echoed by seemingly everyone from contemporary comedians ("I hate the waiting room. Because it's called the waiting room, there's no chance of not waiting. It's built, designed, and intended for waiting. Why would they take you right away when they've got this room all set up?") to Homer Simpson (who begrudgingly lamented the mandatory "waiting period" before purchasing a firearm because "I'm angry now!")

One approach is as follows. In contrast to traffic on the George Washington Bridge, Miriam's wait by the Nile wasn't merely passive downtime, waiting for life to unfold. To the contrary, Rav Elyashiv, *zt"l*, explains[25] that Miriam's *bitachon* in Hashem did not waiver one iota, thereby enabling her to "wait" with the palpable anticipation that a Divinely ordained "exit strategy" would *surely* present itself any minute now. Despite all the odds, Miriam harbored an optimistic outlook and a heart brimming with anticipation. Buoyed by her unflappable *bitachon*, Miriam never budged from her staunch conviction that (as unlikely as it may have seemed), Hashem was indeed orchestrating His Divine Plan for Moshe (in particular) and Am Yisrael (en masse).

Perhaps this is why the Torah "bothers" to record Miriam's seemingly insignificant "waiting" by the riverside. Perhaps this is why, years

Bitachon is the catalyst to transform passive waiting into proactive anticipation.

---

25   Commentary on *Sotah* 11a.

later, the entire Am Yisrael would reciprocate and "wait" for Miriam. Far from being a "most useless place," the waiting of a *ma'amin*—of a Yid who feels "no reason to despair when we see the situation deteriorating"[26]—presents a rare and precious opportunity to find Hashem in our daily lives.

When we know Hashem is part of the unfolding drama of life, we can eagerly and proactively "wait" for the next act rather than passively retreat to that vortex of inertia and non-productivity that is the hallmark of the "Waiting Place."

---

26   Rabbi David Ashear, *Living Emunah* (Artscroll, 2014), p. 66.

Va'eira

The Delight of Normalcy

This thought emerges from, of all people, the stranger who I met unexpectedly and ever so briefly at the end of my driveway one winter morning. While I was leaving for shul, the garbage man (or "sanitation worker," as he might prefer to be called) remarked, "What a nice day it is"—an unanticipated, upbeat comment from a man collecting trash at six-thirty a.m. in dark, damp thirty-seven-degree temperature. How strong could this guy's java possibly be to maintain (and express) such a positive perspective under such seemingly dismal conditions?

The answer, obvious enough, was the fact that this morning's "balmy" weather was a marked departure from the single-digit freeze wave that had gripped Monsey during the previous weeks.

Call it the theory of relativity. Call it the power of contrast. Whatever formal name the experts have labeled this phenomenon, thirty-seven degrees is a whole lot more pleasant when one can still keenly recall yesterday's windchill in their bones.

To some degree or other, we have all experienced that surge of contentedness that invariably accompanies the removal of aggravation. We once spent a Shabbos in a home where the oven beeped every minute, thereby disrupting just about any vestige of restfulness. When, *finally*, eventually, the beeping halted, the ensuing silence was so satiating it called for *Hallel.*

Ever been on a plane two rows behind an infant who's crying at the top of his little lungs. (It's moments like those that one realizes why the FAA bans passengers from carrying firearms). Then, suddenly, when the li'l guy has miraculously calmed down and the passengers (especially the parents) breathe a collective sigh of relief, we inevitably find ourselves that much more appreciative of our surroundings. Did anything really go *right*? You're still cramped on leg space. You're still awaiting the peanuts. Ah, but at least there's quiet. How golden is that silence.

In a nutshell, life becomes increasingly more fulfilling as we realize how little we truly lack.

Life becomes increasingly more fulfilling as we realize how little we truly lack.

This perspective figures prominently in our mindset as Jews. Many of our morning *berachos*, for instance, accentuate the immense gifts we possess by juxtaposing them with the woefulness of a life bereft of those very gifts. Hence, we don't just thank Hashem for vision, but rather praise Hashem for "giving sight to the *blind*." The ability to get out of bed, get dressed, and simply move about our day doesn't seem like much to write home about *until* we consider (and articulate) the challenges, frustrations, and *tzaros* associated with *not* having those gifts.

Rewind a few thousand years. Can you imagine the euphoric relief of the Egyptian population when the frogs finally stopped their incessant, nationwide croaking? I envision that first frog-free morning and its impact on the Mitzri populace. "Yeah, the traffic in Cairo is dreadful today, but at least there are no frogs." "Yeah, the price of *chummus* is going through the roof, but anything's better than those slimy toads everywhere."

Just normal is just great.

And that morning *after* the swarm of wild beasts departed, wouldn't life as "normal" be a reason to smile. After all, no wild boars breathing down my neck. No deadly scorpions or Siberian tigers on the prowl. Just normal is just great.

Therefore, say to the Children of Israel: "I am Hashem, and [1] I shall take you out from under the burdens of Egypt; [2] I shall rescue you from their service; [3] I shall redeem you with an outstretched arm and with great judgments. [4] I shall take you to Me for a people and I shall be a G-d to you; and you shall know that I am Hashem your G-d Who takes you out from under the burdens of Egypt."[27]

In case you are feeling an inexplicable urge to lean to the left, you are correct, these four expressions of liberation correspond to the Four Cups of wine we consume at the Pesach Seder.

Rabbeinu Bachya explains that the very first expression, "I shall take you out," signifies G-d's removal of the Jews from the burdens of slavery even though they would remain as the Egyptians' chattel for another six months. What kind of half-baked, watered-down notion of freedom is this? We are not free to flee Egyptian borders and are already hoisting wine in celebration?

One answer could be that *relatively* speaking, the cessation from backbreaking servitude was indeed a watershed transformation in the lives of Am Yisrael. This initial stage of redemption was euphoric to the extent it marked a radical departure from the bitterness of decades upon decades of physical and emotional burdens. Are we home free? For sure not. Do we have what to rejoice over? One hundred percent.

Carrying this notion into our everyday lives, on those days when we "can't complain," take a moment to appreciate how beautiful the view is from emotional and physical sea level. The *mere* fact that you are not

---

27   *Shemos* 6:6–7.

in the hospital. That you have a closet full of clothes. The *mere* fact that so many things are *not* going wrong. The myriad number of hassles you *don't* have to contend with. These milestones are all too often lost in the shuffle of everyday life. When we take them to heart, our capacity for gratefulness and positivity will undoubtedly be closer at hand.

Bo

New and
Improved

Having failed to make first cuts with the University of
Pennsylvania baseball team (another story for another
time) and having quickly tired of the Ultimate Frisbee club
(how much time can you spend throwing a plastic disc
around), I eventually found myself perched in the starters' gate atop
Tussey Mountain's slalom course, where I (among others) would be com-
peting on behalf of the University's ski club. While Tussey Mountain,
boasting a whopping seven trails and a death-defying vertical drop of
five hundred feet, ain't exactly the Rockies, the hill would have its way
with me that afternoon.

You see, my hopes of navigating the slalom course gracefully, flaw-
lessly, and swiftly were immediately dashed by the cold, icy reality of
the cold, icy snow underfoot. Apparently, the dozens and dozens of
racers before me had carved out a frozen path, thereby rendering the
course more akin to a bobsled run than a ski slope. Fresh snow was
nonexistent. Turning? Forget about it. Basically, it was just about ice
and gravity and prayer. Any hopes of uncorking a "new" trajectory
through those slalom gates was simply impossible given the rigid
grooves left in the wake of my predecessors.

> *This month shall be for you the beginning of the months, it shall be for you the first of the months of the year.*[28]

The capacity for newness is one of life's most valuable treasures. It enables us to embark upon a fresh course, unburdened by the disappointments of previous attempts. It enables sports teams to start a new, fresh season without the blemishes and disappointments of last year's losses. It empowers notetakers to start each page fresh—with neat penmanship and organized ideas—notwithstanding the fact that the notes at the bottom of the previous page are scatterbrained and virtually illegible.

On a broader scale, the capacity for newness is a powerhouse, an X factor that can metamorphize virtually any facet of your life. When your fill-in-the-blank (relationship(s), profession, Shabbos, davening, exercise routine, or learning) has gone stale, a shot of *chiddush* is the most potent antidote for such common ailments as inertia, boredom, ho-hum-ness, and the "same-old same-old" syndrome.

With "newness" one can break out of inertia and forge new pathways in *avodas Hashem.*

Given the immense capacity that lies in a world of *chiddush*, it is no wonder that the celebration of Rosh Chodesh was the very first mitzvah given to Am Yisrael in Mitzrayim. Similarly, it is no wonder that Rabbeinu Yonah identified the first step in *teshuvah* as "casting off one's past" with the conviction that "today your life begins anew!"

As our lives unfold, we need not be shackled to the icy groove of the past. Rather, armed with a healthy dosage of "newness," one can forge unchartered pathways in one's *avodas Hashem.* You're not anchored to the same Shabbos of the past. You're not whetted to the same davening of yesteryear. Your *chessed* need not be perfunctory. Your relationships need not remain on cruise control. To the contrary, "newness" and the innate *simchah* attendant therein awaits those bold enough to pursue it.

---

28   *Shemos* 12:2.

Beshalach

Arrivals and Departures

"Totty," my five-year-old recently inquired en route to school, "Why is our little car traveling on a yellow road instead of a pink road?" Our portable GPS, you see, offers two functions. As a default position, it depicts your vehicle traveling through whatever neighborhood you are in and provides a map of the streets and avenues in your immediate vicinity. In this mode, the screen shows your car traveling on a yellow road. If, however, you enter the coordinates of a specific destination, then the screen depicts your vehicle traveling along a pink road. "Well, Mordechai, good question. You see, we didn't enter a destination into the GPS."

"Well, why don't we?"

"Good point," I responded. "Because this time, we already know where we're going."

This brief exchange reminded me how much hinges on having clarity as to our destination(s) in life. Regardless of one's sophistication, irrespective of one's industriousness, and notwithstanding one's creativity, the extent to which our potential will be actualized depends largely on the degree to which we can identify and articulate our life's mission. For those who

51

maintain a clear vision of where they are headed in life, resources (spiritual, mental, physical, financial, and emotional) can be effectively harnessed to achieve those goals. On the flip side, those who lack that fixity of purpose will invariably find valuable personal resources flittered away.

That being said, one cannot deny how sometimes, the *arrival* at a particular destination pales in significance to the *journey* itself. For instance, "Fly Without Fear" was an organization that offered a program to systematically assuage clients' debilitating fears and anxiety associated with air travel. The program culminated in a "graduation" flight from New York's JFK to New York's LaGuardia airports. Now, one need not be Magellan to realize that there are more efficient ways to travel the ten miles that separate the two locations (even with traffic on the Van Wyck). So why bother with the flight? (And no, it's not for the peanuts and the in-flight martini). The answer is simple: there is something much greater to be gained by this voyage, i.e., the conquering of one's fears, than the mere destination itself.

On similar lines, every Pesach I take my kids for a trip on the Long Island Rail Road. Again, the destination is entirely irrelevant (be it Hicksville or Port Jefferson) because the purpose of the endeavor is not the arrival, but the "getting there." The excitement of the conductor's rapid-fire hole-punching of your ticket. Guessing which commuter will fall asleep next. Watching the Long Island streets whir past. It's about wholesome family bonding, not about beating rush hour.

They arrived at Eilim, where there were twelve springs of water and seventy date-palms; they encamped there by the water.[29]

---

29   *Shemos* 15:27.

They journeyed from Eilim...and the entire assembly of the Children of Israel complained against Moshe and Aharon in the Wilderness.

Rashi: "Because the bread that they took out of Egypt was finished."[30]

The entire assembly of the Children of Israel journeyed from the Wilderness...they encamped in Rephidim and there was no water for the people to drink.[31]

What's going on here?! Who booked this caterer and how come we are sorely lacking in basic supplies such as bread and water? Am I to believe that Hashem, having dismantled Mitzrayim—and, in so doing, having demonstrated total control over every facet of nature—can't also provide a continental breakfast along the way? You miraculously brought swarms of every beast in the animal kingdom to Mitzrayim during the plague of *Arov* and I can't get a simple bagel with cream cheese?!

The answer is self-evident. The odyssey of Am Yisrael in the Wilderness was not so much about getting to their destination, but rather in the lessons and awareness to be gained via the travels along the way. Lessons in *emunah* and *bitachon* (via the *mahn*). Teachings in how to rely on the wise counsel of our leaders. Training in being satisfied with one's lot. An education in learning to live with less. These and many more, which would essentially become the core curriculum for the Jewish People to study and inculcate for all eternity.

We all know these experiences. When we opt for the scenic route precisely because it's scenic (even if it's not necessarily efficient). When we choose to bake that cake *with* the little ones precisely because of the fun of it (even thought it will take three times as long and generate double the mess). The key, of course, is to realize that every destination and every means of getting there has a particular purpose and a specific message to be acquired and internalized.

---

30   Ibid. 16:1–2.
31   Ibid. 17:1–2.

So it is with the Divine GPS that shepherds us, All-Knowingly and All-Lovingly, through life. Some destinations are clearly more pleasant than others. And yet all are purposeful. Some trips are more aggravating than others. And yet none are random. May we merit to appreciate both the "arriving" and the "getting there" of our life's journeys and may Hashem continue to shepherd His Beloved flock to pastures where we can grow and thrive and live fully.

Every destination and every leg of the journey has its particular purpose and its specific lesson for life.

Yisro

From Sinai with Love

Hashem's Divine Revelation at Har Sinai and Am Yisrael's acceptance of the Torah was the single greatest event in the history of mankind. However, those who know their stuff are aware of at least two other momentous occasions where Am Yisrael received the Torah anew, namely:

- The first Yom Kippur where the Torah was "reaccepted" amid an atmosphere of sincere *teshuvah*
- Generations hence, during the times of Mordechai HaTzaddik and Queen Esther, when the Torah was "reaccepted" in the wake of the miraculous rescue of the Jewish People from the crosshairs of Haman's "Final Solution"

What was unique about Am Yisrael's "renewed" commitment to the Torah during the Purim epoch? In the terse words of Chazal, this new commitment to Torah was fueled by *ahavah*.

About ten years ago, we made our annual delivery of *mishlo'ach manos* to various rabbis, *talmidei chachamim*, and *roshei yeshiva* as part and parcel of the Purim festivities. All the while, I kept one inquiry in my back

55

pocket and optimistically yearned for an appropriate time to ask (and be answered) amid the whirlwind of Purim, a day that rarely allows for quiet moments of introspection.

Lo and behold, when I visited Rabbi Yisroel Rokowsky, my Rosh Yeshiva, his home was surprisingly quiet, as the onslaught of visitors and students of all ages had not yet begun to trickle in. Here was my golden opportunity. "Rosh Yeshiva," I asked, "what's the difference between accepting the Torah at Sinai and accepting the Torah *out of love* during the days of Mordechai and Esther? After all, it's the same Torah. Same verses. Same mitzvos. At the end of the day, what's the real gain?"

In his inimitable style, he guided me to a profound answer à la left field.

"Do you like baseball?" the Rosh Yeshiva inquired.

"Well, I used to be into it more… Less so nowadays."

"Did you root for the Mets or Yankees?"

"Mets."

"When was the peak of your interest?"

"I would say 1986, 1987, thereabouts."

"OK, who played first base?"

"Keith Hernandez."

"Second base?"

"Wally Backman."

"Third base?"

"Ray Knight"

…And so it went, as I proceeded to rattle off the entire infield, outfield, and pitching staff as if I were reading it off an old newspaper.

Now, what exactly the 1986 Mets had to do with Purim was way beyond me (and I was still sober). Little did I realize it, but Rabbi Rokowsky had led me right to the crux of the matter. He then asked, "When was the last time you thought about that?"

"Uh. I don't know, five years, ten years…not for a *long* time."

"There's your answer," he explained. "That's the difference. The reason you recalled it so quickly and clearly, the reason that information was at your fingertips, the reason that knowledge became a part of you…is *because you took to it out of love!* And that is the difference between accepting the Torah out of love."

Ever hear part of a song while waiting on line in the bank—a song you haven't heard in ages—and you instantaneously and effortlessly start singing its words? I suppose the very same explanation applies. Those lyrics were downloaded onto your mental and emotional hard drive out of love. And so, they remain on file for years to come. Even though we're constantly forgetting infinitely more important things like our PIN codes, anniversary, what the Rabbi had to say in shul, or what *berachah* to make on a blueberry.

The study of Torah and our attempt to implement its timeless laws, morals, and values into our lives is a lifelong endeavor for each and every member of Am Yisrael. We seek to fulfill the same 613 mitzvos. We read the same *parashiyos*. We study the same *sefarim*. We daven the same *tefillos*.

What separates one person's rote observance from another's heartfelt dedication often boils down to whether or not an X factor exists (and if so, to what degree). That X factor is Love. Love of Hashem. Love of His Torah. Love of His People. And the concomitant deep-seated appreciation for the opportunity to serve Hashem—and not *just* to serve, but to do so out of love.

As Yidden, we are encouraged (perhaps expected) to reaccept the Torah each and every day with renewed enthusiasm. To this end, every morning our davening includes a request to Hashem to "instill in our hearts to understand…to listen, learn, teach…and fulfill all the words of Your Torah…" And not just ho-hum, but "with love." Who can estimate the gains to be acquired by pouring some additional emotional octane into those words?

> Love is the X factor that separates rote observance from heartfelt dedication.

For when our acceptance of the Torah is infused with love, it can permeate our beings—our heart, mind, and soul—to a greater degree, and thereby boost the efforts we are already undertaking, elevating them to a truly inspiring "labor of love."

Mishpatim

You'll Never Walk Alone

S everal summers ago, our house was somehow designated as a drop-off site for new school supplies that would ultimately be distributed to financially strapped families whose budgets simply could not absorb the significant costs associated with outfitting one's children with brand new backpacks, binders, composition notebooks, glue sticks (and beyond) for the rapidly approaching academic year. In yet another testament to the expansiveness of the Jewish heart, supplies of all sorts poured in—markers and No. 2 pencils, dividers and reinforcements.

To our surprise, one particular woman dropped off loads and loads of supplies. While we knew her to be a very generous soul, this particular display of generosity caught us somewhat off guard because she herself did not boast *such* a robust income to be lavishly doling out gifts to others. After her third trip from her car, she mentioned how this particular cause struck such a soft spot in her heart. Why? "Because I remember that one August, when *my* kids were young and we simply didn't have the money for school supplies. I remember the pain and disappointment of breaking the news to my kids that there would be no new marker sets this year. Even though the kids understood, as a parent it felt just awful. So now that our kids are grown and our own financial means are, *baruch Hashem*, not so tight, I wanted to give a little bit more.

"Perhaps a little additional effort from my end can spare some mother somewhere the heartache of telling *her* child that she has to get by with last year's binder (even though its way out of style). You know, for kids it's a big thing. Especially when all her classmates have new things."

When you will lend money to My people, to the poor person who is with you, do not act toward him as a creditor, do not place interest upon him.

Rashi: "The poor person who is with you—Look at yourself as if you are the poor person."[32]

Our life's journeys are singular and unique. Along the way we suffer "slings and arrows" and challenges that, if internalized properly, provide each of us with a personal, vivid "emotional vocabulary" to process life—not just our own, but others' lives as well. One person endures loneliness. Others struggle with regret and are plagued perpetually with second-guessing. Some grapple with debilitating guilt on a daily basis. Others' spirits are routinely torpedoed by low self-esteem or self-doubt. One endures difficult financial straits and the spectrum of associated stresses and frustrations. Others live lives complicated by relationships that flounder (at best) and are downright dysfunctional (at worst).

Extract emotional know-how from your own *life's challenges in order to understand (and enrich) the lives of others.*

True, no two chapters are ever truly identical. (Indeed, professing to know *exactly* what someone else is going through rarely strikes the intended chord of empathy.) That being said, the Torah's notion of alleviating another's *tzaros* (in this case, financial hardship) demands more than the perfunctory act of cutting a check. Seemingly, parting of one's own hard-earned money is just the first step. Beyond that, the Torah adjures us to reach into our hearts

32   *Shemos* 24:24.

and minds—not just our wallets—in our responsibility toward others. To dispel not just poverty, but the attendant loneliness as well. To buoy not just their finances, but their forlorn spirits as well.

Our lives teach volumes to those of us attuned to learning from the past. Beyond that, opportunities abound to apply those very teachings for those driven to walk in the ways of Hashem.

Terumah

Golden Opportunities

It will be a great day when our schools have all the money they need, and our air force has to have a bake sale to buy a bomber.

Robert Fulghum, author of All I Really Need to Know
I Learned in Kindergarten

Keruvim—they each had the image of a child's face.[33]

During one of his travels, the great Rav Meir Shapiro, *zt"l*, happened upon a city wherein the network of Torah educational institutions had been sorely neglected. Regretfully, it was readily apparent that the *chinuch* of the future generations occupied a distant second (or third or fourth) among the residents' priorities. When Rav Shapiro inquired further as to why their schools were in such a lamentable state, he was told that the community was not

---

33   Rashi to *Shemos* 25:18.

particularly well-off financially and was simply "doing the best it could" in light of the various demands that the populace was shouldering.

However, upon arriving at the city's shul, Rav Shapiro was struck by the grandeur, elegance, and dignity of a building that certainly appeared as if no expense had been spared. Struck by the disparity between the lavish shul and the overlooked yeshiva, Rav Shapiro could not turn a blind eye to this error in communal judgment.

When he ascended the bimah on Shabbos morning—*parashas Terumah*—to offer his *derashah*, he opened with a riddle based on the Gemara in *Menachos* (28b): All of the vessels listed in conjunction with the construction of the *Mishkan*—the *Menorah*, the *Shulchan*, the *Aron*, etc.—can be fashioned from silver (or even less precious metals) in the event that gold (the preferred way of doing so) was not available. All, except for one.

"The *Keruvim*," Rav Shapiro explained, "which sit atop the *Aron*, must be fashioned out of gold." The use of any other metal, even silver, is insufficient and—worse—runs afoul of the *aveirah* of fashioning a false deity.

"Why is that? What's unique about the *Keruvim*?" Rav Shapiro pondered aloud, as his heretofore veiled reproof of the community's priorities was coming to surface. "Because the *Aron* is where the Torah is kept, and perched atop the *Aron* is the image of a child's face…to remind us that when it comes to educating the younger generation of Am Yisrael, *nothing less than gold will suffice!*"

At the end of the day, regardless of the excuse, *chinuch ha'banim* is simply *way* too important to skimp on, marginalize, or hope to just "get by" with the bare minimum.

To the contrary, part and parcel of our identity as the People of the Book has been the paramount importance placed upon *chinuch* and the associated accountability to ensure the transfer of the Torah's wisdom, depth, joyfulness, meaning, and downright *geshmak* to the next generation (and beyond).

From a prioritization standpoint, I often wonder if I'm giving my absolute all to whomever I have the merit to teach (younger or older, related or not, observant or not-yet-observant, overwhelmed or under-inspired, passionate, perplexed, or downright apathetic). When

I walk through my front door and who-knows-how-much-homework awaits on the other side, am I *really* capitalizing on this golden opportunity to participate in my children's Torah education? Am I mustering the requisite degree of focus, patience, and enthusiasm—or would I rather just unwind at the end of a gauntlet of a day?

Are we helping to bring the Torah to life, pulling out all the stops to ensure that the *simchah* of a Torah life is implanted in the generations to come, or are we simply "getting the job done" while rifling through the mail and fielding phone calls (and emails and texts)?

When it comes to *chinuch*, are we delivering our very best or just getting by?

Rav Shapiro's words ring true for us more than ever. Not just when it comes to earmarking funds for tuition, tutors, etc. but beyond the dollars and cents. Are we properly discharging the awesome responsibility, opportunity, and yes, privilege, to see that our children—and all our "students"—receive nothing less than the gold standard of every facet of our innate capacities as "teachers."

We must see to it that the *chinuch* we give is golden—it may very well be the best investment we'll ever make.

Tetzaveh

Kick the Habit

A s the blissfulness of a young couple's marriage began to dissipate amid aggravation, quarrelsomeness, and disharmony, they valiantly sought out the advice and counsel of various marriage counselors. No one could seemingly right the ship that appeared to be on a crash course for separation and divorce. As multiple counseling sessions failed to yield any headway, one of their rabbinic advisors suggested that, as a last-ditch effort, they take the matter to one of the most senior leaders of the Jewish People, Rav Chaim Pinchas Scheinberg, *zt"l*.

With decades of Torah wisdom, life experience, and a razor-sharp understanding of the human condition (and our foibles), Rav Scheinberg exhausted every angle before he, too, ultimately conceded that perhaps severing the relationship was the only viable exit strategy. However, before deciding the fate of their union, he concluded that they should wait two weeks, during which they should engage in self-contemplation and—unexpectedly—watch their own wedding video on multiple occasions.

Lo and behold, when they reconvened two weeks later, a heretofore undetectable ray of hope began to glimmer from amid the abyss of hopelessness and helplessness. Somehow, that emotional core that remained beyond the reach of skilled marriage counselors was rendered (somewhat) accessible via the videographers' captured moments of the *bedeken*, the *chuppah*, the ring, the breaking of the glass, the mazel tovs, and, of course, the optimism and enthusiasm that surged when everyone "put hands together…for the *very* first time…Mr. and Mrs.…." Getting back to basics enabled them to refocus and reorient themselves so that the troublesome patterns that had developed could be assessed in a different light.

True, those initial moments of excitement, happiness, and optimism had been eroded by the realities of everyday life; nevertheless, revisiting them in full living color provided the foundation from which to rebuild, repair, and renew.

It shall be on Aharon's forehead…always, for appeasement for them before Hashem.

Rashi: *"It teaches that he shall touch it while it is on his forehead so that he should not remove his consciousness from it."*[34]

You shall offer…a continual olah-offering for your generations, at the entrance of the Tent of Meeting, before Hashem; where I will arrange audience for you to speak to you there.

Rashi: *"From day to day and there should not be an intervening day without it."*[35]

This day, Hashem, Your G-d, commands you…

Rashi: *"On each day, they should be new in your eyes, as if you were commanded regarding them that day."*[36]

This day you have become a people.

Rashi: *"Every day [the commandments] shall be in your eyes as if you had entered the covenant with Him that day."*[37]

---

34   *Shemos* 28:38.
35   Ibid. 29:41.
36   *Devarim* 26:16.
37   Ibid. 27:9.

One of the greatest challenges associated with Hashem's gracious and gratuitous outpouring of perpetual blessings is the wherewithal not to lose sight of how good things truly are. The increasing number of activities to complete, obligations to discharge, and car pools to execute—all indicia of a "full" life—invariably divert our attention away from the pure joy of being alive.

Even if we haven't hit the lottery, doesn't the "everyday routine" provide ample opportunity to reflect upon and internalize a genuine and deep-seated outlook of *hakaras ha'tov*?

All the doctors we *didn't* need to see.

All the prescriptions we *didn't* need filled.

All the drivers that *didn't* rear-end us.

All the nights we *didn't* go to sleep hungry.

And we haven't even begun to tally all the bills that got paid, all the food that was consumed, all the weddings we danced at, and all the times we arrived at our destination safe and sound...

Since our mind can easily rattle off dozens and dozens of "everyday" Divine "gifts," why are we not brimming with gratitude? Why does our baseline attitude so frequently overlook all these undeserved riches? Why are we not eager to serve Hashem "out of an abundance of everything"?[38] Rav Miller, *zt"l*, identifies a primary culprit as none other than—habit.

While habit can be advantageous, i.e., when davening with a minyan becomes part and parcel of one's daily routine; or when your tefillin can practically wrap themselves while you're mentally out to lunch (at least until your coffee kicks in), it can (and often does) wreak havoc on our capacity to truly appreciate that which is already good in our lives.

> Habit can wreak havoc on our capacity to truly appreciate the abundant goodness that is ever present in our lives.

We, as Jews, occupy a singular place on the world's stage. We are uniquely equipped (and expected) to perceive and express Hashem's wisdom, plan, purpose, might, and kindliness. When cued up properly, those blessings that are

---

38   Ibid. 28:47.

so frequently overlooked can amount to a perpetual song of praise and gratitude to Hashem. When we shed the blinders of habit and reawaken ourselves to the innate goodness in our days, a heightened awareness of Hashem's abundant kindness awaits.

Ki Sisa

Coin of the Realm

While championing mankind's capacity for creativity, a noted playwright related one particularly memorable theatrical performance. From a location standpoint, the play's director had staged his rendition of a Shakespearian play on the shore of an aesthetic lake somewhere in the English countryside. From a timing standpoint, the drama was choreographed such that its conclusion would coincide precisely with a majestic sunset over the tranquil water. Thus, when the very last character delivered his very last line, the actor turned away from the audience and proceeded to run *into* the water behind him. Little did anyone know, but small platforms had been submerged right below the water such that this actor could literally disappear out over the lake into the horizon amid the splendor of the setting sun. A showstopper indeed.

What made this choreography particularly noteworthy was that the *text* of the play merely stated "Exit stage." Ho-hum. What could be more plain vanilla than that? Surely doesn't mention anything about dramatic dashes into watery sunsets. Indeed, in the four hundred years since Shakespeare's passing, dozens and dozens of directors have sought to transform his two-dimensional words into three-dimensional life. Behold, what this one creative director envisioned when he double-clicked on the seemingly simple, plain, banal words of "Exit stage."

This is what they shall give—everyone who passes among the counted—half of the shekel...to Hashem.

Rashi: "G-d showed Moshe a sort of coin of fire whose weight was half a shekel and told him give a coin like this."[39]

Moshe was perplexed and could not understand the essence of the mitzvah of the giving of the half-shekel...[until]...Hashem brought forth the likeness of a fiery coin from underneath His Throne and showed it to Moshe saying, "This is the coin they shall give."[40]

Reish Lakish said: It was revealed and known before the One whose word created the world that Haman would ultimately weigh out shekalim in order to attain the consent of Achashveirosh to destroy the Jewish Nation. Hashem therefore preceded their shekalim to his...[41]

What was so complicated about this seemingly straightforward, uncomplicated half-shekel donation that Moshe seemingly failed to comprehend? And, furthermore, what's the connection between the *shekalim* that Am Yisrael brought in the Wilderness and Haman's *shekalim* centuries later?

The commentaries identify two pervasive shortcomings found in Am Yisrael in the years preceding Haman's rise to power. First, we were a fragmented nation suffering from disunity. Second, we discharged our religious obligations in a ho-hum, cruise-control, another-day-another-davening, "sleepy" fashion. The mitzvah of the half-shekel possesses

39   *Shemos* 30:13.
40   *Yerushalmi, Shekalim*, ch 1.
41   *Megillah* 13.

a unique capacity to address (and strengthen) those two weaknesses. [N.B. This is one of the several reasons why *parashas Shekalim* is read as a precursor to Purim.]

Each and every member of Am Yisrael (regardless of their tax bracket) was obligated to donate the *exact* same currency, earmarked for the *exact* same expenditures (i.e., the communal *korbanos*), and each contributed only a *half*-shekel (as opposed to a whole one). This being the case, the mitzvah underscored one's sense of camaraderie with his fellow Yidden, thereby diluting the lingering sense of disparateness and disharmony.

The notion of the "fiery coin" shown to Moshe Rabbeinu spoke not to *what* the mitzvah is or *how* the coin was intended to look—for neither of those details were particularly confusing. Rather, the Divine PowerPoint demonstration was designed to show *how* (emotionally) the mitzvah should be fulfilled—i.e., with a fiery, impassioned yearning to accept and appreciate one's rank among Am Yisrael and the obligations associated therewith. In this respect, even the seemingly bland act of contributing a half-shekel (whoop-de-doo), which could have been discharged in a two-dimensional, mindless, ritual fashion, presented an opportunity to serve Hashem with brimming enthusiasm.

One mitzvah. One coin. You choose how much fire to pour into it. It can be given mindlessly—like a toll on the Garden State Parkway—or you can give it with a heart full of gusto, generating a sincere sense of unity among Yidden, while fending off the forces of apathy.

Anyone can simply "exit stage." Fortunate are those who can take the (seemingly) everyday and propel it to the heights of connectivity to Hashem. Haman underestimated the emotional depth and spiritual meaningfulness that lay hidden within our *shekalim*. Then, and now, the *machatzis ha'shekel* testifies to our individual and national capacity to elevate the mundane.

> Fortunate are those who can take the everyday and propel it to the heights of connectivity to Hashem.

Vayakhel

Above and Beyond

O ur family was (yet again) on the receiving end of countless *berachos* as our infant, Yosef Chaim, underwent surgery and, *baruch Hashem*, all had gone well. Hashem's kindness was apparent at every turn—the absence of traffic en route to Manhattan (well, it was four a.m.), a (reasonably) affordable spot in a nearby garage, a team of selfless, dedicated, and tireless grandparents holding down the home front and caring for siblings of all ages. Among all these heroes, though, we would be remiss if two unlikely heroes went unsung in the whirlwind of postoperative life.

The bubble-maker: While reviewing various preoperative protocols with the presiding medical team and nursing staff, a young woman introduced herself as a "Child Life Specialist." This staff-member's role in the equation? To pull out all the stops in a valiant (albeit remote) attempt to entertain little Yosef Chaim. Within minutes of meeting our son, she transformed our rather bland, spartan waiting room into a virtual playpen, with an area for our son to play amid an impressive array of rattles, toys, balls, and stuffed animals she provided. When Yosef tired of that (give the guy a *little* credit—he had been fasting for several hours by now), this Child Life Specialist broke out the Curious George paraphernalia. When the allure of the curious monkey and the Man in the Yellow Hat waned, our room was cascaded with...of all things, bubbles. Yes—nothing like a wand and soapy water to mesmerize a starving infant on the verge of surgery (not to mention his sleep-deprived parents). I cannot tell you what a relief these bubbles brought to us all.

Fast-forward a few hours and little Yosef, bloody but unbowed from the surgery, was slowly shaking off the anesthesia. Not a happy camper to be sure. With Mommy and Daddy trying everything in the books to appease, entertain, soothe, or distract him, who came to the rescue? None other than the bubbly bubble-maker. Yosef was relieved. The parents exhaled (finally). And the entire postoperative wing at NYU was ecstatic that the once hysterical infant was now relatively serene.

The keepers of the Bikur Cholim room: The other individual(s) to whom we owe a debt of gratitude are those anonymous, benevolent souls responsible for the upkeep of the Bikur Cholim room. Besides providing a quiet, peaceful place to daven that morning (separate and apart from the frenetic hallways and cramped waiting rooms), its confines were a wall-to-wall testament to the Jewish capacity for kindliness. Fridges stocked to the hilt with sandwiches of all types. Microwaves (separate ones for milchig and fleishig, of course). Phone chargers. *Sefarim*. Magazines. And a host of numbers to call if you are in need of anything from a local apartment to a Shabbos meal to a tasty salt-and-pepper kugel. What my life would have looked like without their coffee, one can only fathom.

What's the point of all this?

The point is that the physical plant of NYU Hospital would have been state of the art and virtually self-sufficient *without* the Bikur Cholim room serving as an oasis of Yiddishkeit for anyone looking to revitalize their soul (or a kosher turkey sandwich).

The point is that the vast human resources of NYU Hospital would have been more than adequate *without* a Child Life Specialist on staff.

I am sure the surgeon has a better parking space than the "overseer" of the Bikur Cholim room.

I am sure the anesthesiologist's paycheck far exceeds that of the Child Life Specialist.

I am positive there are loads of elaborate medical equipment on hand and an abundance of sophisticated medications…and we (hopefully) appreciate them all…But if you ask these parents, the experience would have been *vastly* different without that quiet room to pray and without that soapy water that produced those bubbles that soothed our little Yosef Chaim.

And the work was sufficient for all the work, to do it—and having a surplus.[42]

This seemingly self-contradictory verse is the subject of much discussion in the classical commentaries. After all, when the materials collected for the construction of the *Mishkan* were tallied up, was it a "sufficient" amount (i.e., just enough) or "having a surplus" (i.e., above and beyond what was necessary)?

At a basic level, perhaps the Torah is alerting us to the notion that for the *Mishkan* to simply function, bare minimums would have sufficed: a *Menorah*, a *Mizbei'ach* (or two), curtains, walls, clothing for the *Kohanim*, etc. Just like a hospital could conceivably get by with the bare minimums. However, Hashem's Divine blueprint for the *Mishkan* called for much *more* than was necessary. Its vessels glistened with gold and silver. Ornate walls. Curtains depicting master craftsmanship with every stitch. Garments of turquoise and purple. Precious gemstones.

Did the *Mishkan* really *need* gold beaten into thin sheets and cut into strands such that one strand of gold could be spun together with turquoise wool, purple wool, scarlet wool, and twisted flax? Why not just put up some faux cedarwood panels, a felt curtain, and get the services underway?!

In short, Hashem bestowed upon His beloved Am Yisrael a *Mishkan* that was both "sufficient" to accomplish its function and also laden with an abundance of "surplus" details left, right, and center. Items that went above and beyond the "essential" for the sole purpose (or soul purpose, as the case may be) of endearing His beloved Yidden and bringing us closer to Him.

---

42   *Shemos* 36:7

Coming full circle, a hospital needn't provide bubbles. It needn't provide a quiet place to daven. Oh...but when it does, how grateful must we be. By extension, Hashem's world could have been stocked with nothing more than the bare essentials necessary for survival. Did we need the colorful autumn foliage or dozens and dozens of luscious fruits of every color and taste? Are majestic, towering mountains and beautiful sunsets *essential*, or rather do they represent one of the myriad instances of Hashem's benevolent desire to enrich our lives with reasons to rejoice? How enchanted can we become with Hashem's glorious world when we take advantage of the priceless opportunity to be dazzled by it—and all its "surplus" details—with fresh, impressionable eyes and ears eager to appreciate our Maker for both that which is "sufficient" and, especially, that which is "surplus."

> Hashem packed His glorious world with "surplus" details for us to enjoy.

Pekudei

Divine GPS

Just a few days prior to Yom Tov, an individual of financial means encountered a rebbetzin whom he knew and held in high esteem. Knowing full well (a) the costs associated with preparing a proper Yom Tov and (b) the financial pressures facing this woman's household, the person respectfully inquired, "Are you OK in terms of Yom Tov?"

On the spot, without hesitation, the woman answered, "Well, we're exactly where Hashem wants us to be." Clearly, her *emunah* and *bitachon* was a palpable, living force in her life—as much as gravity is a palpable, living force in our lives. It was not an abstract theological idea. Rather, it was the prism through which she processed her very existence. The means of confronting the everyday.

This, despite the fact that she had lost a child not too long ago.

This, despite the fact that she had to relinquish a teaching position that she held so dearly.

Surely, if complaining was anywhere on this woman's radar screen, she had plenty of "raw material" to fill her mind, heart, and days with bitterness, sadness, and seemingly well-grounded kvetching.

Moreover, her confident, matter-of-fact, unhesitating response spoke volumes. She felt no need to consult her worn copy of *Shaar Ha'bitachon*. She did not fumble and stumble merely to utter the "party line." To the contrary, she responded with the clarity, confidence, conviction, and optimism of a person who is cognizant of

Hashem's benevolent presence in their life—always and at all times.

> *When the cloud was raised up from upon the Mishkan, the Children of Israel would journey on all their journeys. If the cloud did not rise up, they would not journey, until the day it rose up. For the cloud of Hashem would be on the Mishkan by day, and fire would be on it at night, before the eyes of all the House of Israel in all their journeys.*
>
> *Rashi: "At any stage of the journey that they would travel, the cloud would rest at the place in which they were to encamp."*[43]

Perhaps this is the reason why the Torah[44] bothers to recount each of the myriad stops along Am Yisrael's forty-year sojourn in the Wilderness. Some of the places were lush and pleasant like Eilim, where they were encamped alongside twelve springs. Others were arid and unpleasant like Marah, where there was no water to quench their thirst. Some produced watershed events, like the sending of the spies, and others were marked by the passing of beloved leaders such as Aharon and Miriam. Still others remain mere geographic locations regarding which the Torah does not reveal any further details.

Hashem does not lose track of neshamos; rather at all times, each of us is exactly where He wants us to be.

But to be sure, every single location merited eternal mention in our Eternal Torah for one reason and one reason only—*because they were exactly where Hashem wanted His People to be.* And so too, as Am Yisrael's timeless voyage continues, the Nation and each and every one of us are "exactly where Hashem wants us to be."

We routinely misplace car keys and eyeglasses. Airlines misplace baggage. Parents even misplace children amid the sea of humanity at

---

43 *Shemos* 40:36–38.
44 *Bamidbar* 33.

carnivals or crowded grocery stores. When I was growing up there was even a public service announcement, "It's Nine O'clock—Do You Know Where Your Children Are?"

But Hashem does not "misplace" *neshamos.* To the contrary, each and every member of His beloved family is cherished and accounted for. More than that, at every moment, we are exactly where Hashem wants us to be, and somehow, someway, wherever that place may be, it is surely the best possible place for us. (Regardless if we harbor thoughts to the contrary). When we allow our outlooks and perspectives to be filtered through this prism of purposefulness and Divine design, our happiness will be less vulnerable to the "slings and arrows" of life. Our frustrations may seem less insurmountable. Our sense of confidence will be steeled against that pesky second-guessing that so often takes us out of the moment. For knowing that we're exactly where Hashem wants us to be is indeed the key to rejoicing in the here and now.

Vayikra

The Heart of the Matter

With Shabbos just a couple of hours away, "Passenger," a patron of a local grocery store, respectfully inquired of a fellow Yid (aka "Driver"), "Perhaps you're going my way and could offer me a lift?" Since the destination was more or less on Driver's way, and sensing an opportunity for one last *chessed* before Shabbos, Driver acquiesced, brought his car around, and motioned for Passenger to settle himself (and his assorted bags of groceries) in the backseat.

As they departed from the grocery store's parking lot, Driver choreographed a seamless drop-off "procedure" that struck a delicate balance between Passenger's need to disembark and Driver's concern lest he hold up traffic unnecessarily—especially in light of *erev Shabbos* traffic congestion. With a matter-of-fact demeanor, Driver explained, "You know, Friday afternoon traffic can be quite heavy, and we don't want to tick anyone off by holding up cars behind us. Please, when we approach the stoplight near your destination, be prepared to exit with your groceries lickety-split."

While the plan was relatively straightforward, the execution thereof, needless to say, left much to be desired. Passenger stumbled, fumbled, and bumbled getting out of the car, his cantaloupe tumbled into the street, the heretofore red light turned green and, as expected, pandemonium unfolded. Amid honking horns from frustrated drivers, Passenger attempted to recollect his groceries, Driver became emotionally unglued and started barking commands as to Plan B ("Just get back in and I'll drive you further!") and the cantaloupe—of course—was a goner.

When the dust settled on this unfortunate episode, Driver was left scratching his head in wonderment. What happened here? Why did his benign, benevolent attempt to help a fellow Jew end up in such an unpleasant debacle? While practical solutions were readily apparent, (i.e., next time just disembark on a side street and take some of the variables out of the equation), a macro-explanation was still lacking.

Seeking to clarify the situation (and hopefully glean some constructive criticism), Driver recounted the events to a sage Rabbi, one steeped in the *derech ha'mussar*, in the hopes of discovering a deeper explanation. The Rabbi digested the episode and offered the following diagnosis: "Deep down, Driver, you didn't really want this mitzvah. You didn't really want to extend this *chessed* to this Jew. Maybe you didn't have the heart to decline. Maybe you were too embarrassed to say no. Whatever it may be. For had you *sincerely* desired to assist—right down to your core—you would have merited Divine protection that would have spared you such a fiasco."

It is an olah-offering, a fire-offering, a pleasing fragrance to Hashem.

Rashi: "It says 'a pleasing fragrance' about fowl and it says 'a pleasing fragrance' about livestock, to tell you that one who gives much is the same as one who gives less, as long as his heart is directed toward Heaven."[45]

Virtue is measured not merely by *what* we do, but against the wholeheartedness with which we do it.

---

45   *Vayikra* 1:17

> *You shall surely give to your destitute brother, and let your heart not feel bad when you give him, for in return for this matter, Hashem, your G-d, will bless you in all your deeds and in your every undertaking.*[46]

Many times, the Torah reminds us that mitzvos and conduct are merely a starting point in our *avodas Hashem*. The true measure of piety and virtue, however, is hidden to most (if not all) who simply are not privy to the heart of our matters. In this respect, the caliber of our conduct is measured not only by what we do but with the wholeheartedness with which we do what we do.

Chessed, at any level, is wonderful and worthy of emulation and (usually) well-received. *Ahavas chessed*, however, is an entirely different stratosphere, where those seeking to walk in the path blazed by Avraham Avinu aspire to infuse their "good deeds" with sincere streaks of *rachamim*, empathy, and love.

To the extent we are already well-along in our respective "careers" of *chessed*, self-reflection is certainly warranted to discover where (and how) we can enhance our benevolent actions. As our purity of motive becomes more sincere, so too, we are likely to encounter a heightened sense of Divine protection and assistance.

---

46   *Devarim* 15:10.

Tzav

Torchbearers

Inspired by a particularly stirring *Ne'ilah* service, I bounded home to make the post-Yom Kippur Havdalah for my wife and family. Our candle, however, had gone out during the course of the day and thus I was left without one of the necessary elements for Havdalah, i.e., a flame that had remained lit throughout Yom Kippur. A quick call to our neighbors confirmed that they had such a flame available and I was more than welcome to "borrow" it for the purposes of our Havdalah.

The only problem being, of course, how to transport this fire so that it could keep aflame from their living room to ours. I took one of those colonial glass lanterns, hoping it would do the trick and properly shield the highly sought-after flame from the wind and elements. As my father would say, it turned out to be the "right tool for the right job," and we were able to commence with Havdalah and the post-Yom Kippur break-fast.

Behind the scenes, this innocuous vignette provided a parable that I would hold near and dear for many years to come. For I perceived, in a nutshell, what our life's mission is all about, i.e., transporting the flame of truth and Torah from one generation to the other without it getting snuffed out by foreign elements along the way. Isn't that what our *mesorah* boils down to? An honorable list of great-grandparents and *bubbies* who gave their all emotionally, psychologically, physically, and financially to ensure that the Torah they received from their ancestors is the very Torah that they would give over to the next generation. The same mitzvos. The same *middos*. The same ambitions. The same commitment to *chessed* and concern for others.

> *And Aharon and his sons carried out all the matters that Hashem commanded through Moshe.*[47]
>
> *Rashi: "To tell their praise that they veered neither right nor left."*

One of the many themes that permeates our *avodas Hashem* is our obligation as a link in the chain back to Mitzrayim. Every year since Hashem liberated His beloved nation, Jews of all types have gathered together. Same menu (even the bitter herbs didn't go out of style). Same story (Maxwell House brand is optional). Same four sons. Same four cups. Same leaning. Same *Dayeinu*. I could ask the very four questions at my grandfather's grandfather's Seder and we hope and pray that generations from now, our grandchildren's grandchildren will be equipped to ask—and answer—those very same questions.

Not just dry, two-dimensional answers. But living, breathing, enthusiastic, brimming-with-joyfulness answers. That future, however, depends in large degree upon us...the present. As Rav Dessler wrote in a letter to his students, "One who tries to influence others toward Torah without himself inwardly experiencing the grandeur of Judaism...lives in a world of illusion. Consequently, he will not succeed in influencing them. Only words that come from the heart—from reality—enter into people's hearts."[48]

Enthusiastic appreciation of one's own heritage is essential for those who seek to forge and inspire future links in the *mesorah*.

When we embrace and celebrate our awesome, pristine tradition...

---

47   *Vayikra* 8:36.
48   *Michtav Mi'Elihayu* vol. II, p.63.

When we endeavor to live up to our awesome obligation to pass that tradition along...

We will, with G-d's help, kindle that fire inside us. A desire to understand more, to understand better, to reignite our relationship with Hashem and His People and, in so doing, find that spark that just might kindle future generations of Yidden.

Shemini

Now You See Him...

For those of you who have ever spell-checked a Microsoft Word document, you are familiar with the various options that the program presents. When the spell-checker stops on a term that it perceives as misspelled, one can double-click on either "Ignore Once," "Ignore All," "Add to Dictionary," "Change," or "Change All."

Upon recently completing a document, I launched the spell-checker in the hopes of identifying any pesky typos that had crept in inadvertently. Lo and behold, the program stopped on the word "Hashem" and the computer prompted me to the normal menu of options—and simultaneously offered an idea of immense profundity and vast applicability.

Before my eyes, the screen was offering me the option to, of all things, "Ignore Hashem." More than that, I had the option of ignoring Hashem "Once" or even ignoring Hashem "*Always.*"

> Our mission in this world is to perceive Hashem in as many nooks and crannies of life as possible.

Hold the phone. Forget about spell-check. This is a paradigm for life! A flight plan to accomplish our mission in this world to perceive Hashem in as many nooks and crannies of life as possible. In nature, in history, in all the daily, humdrum occurrences that, when we think about it, are far, far from humdrum. Quite the opposite, to the trained eye, the yearning heart, the inquisitive mind, and the discerning soul, "there is," as Shakespeare put it, "special providence in the fall of a sparrow." And the fall of a government. Sunrise and sunset. The blossoming of the trees. The April showers and the May flowers...

Hashem spoke to Aharon saying: Do not drink intoxicating wine, you and your sons with you, when you come to the Tent of Meeting...this is an eternal decree for your generations. In order to distinguish between the sacred and the profane, and between the contaminated and the pure.[49]

For I am Hashem Who elevates you from the land of Egypt to be a G-d unto you; you shall be holy, for I am holy.[50]

And from the great and open miracles, a person shall admit to the "hidden" miracles that constitute the foundation of the entire Torah...[51]

After the four questions have been answered, the four cups consumed, and the four sons off to bed; after we all "know one," have at least one *charoses*-stained garment to send to the cleaners, and have torpedoed our carbs-free diet via matzah overload—what is *the* (or at least *a*) take-home message from Passover that we can internalize, perhaps even after the taste of the afikomen has dissipated from our palate?

As the *Ramban*[52] enumerates, the mission is to somehow bridge the gap between the open miracles of blood, boils, and darkness and the more "natural" miracles of our own bloodstream, skin, and the sunlight. To script our *own* stanzas to our *own* personal *Dayeinu*, whereby that

---

49   *Vayikra* 10:8–10.
50   Ibid. 11:45.
51   *Ramban, Shemos* 13:16.
52   Ibid.

which is so often overlooked or taken for granted (e.g., waking up pain-free, having a roof over one's head, or a fridge full of food) can take on a significance nothing short of miraculous.

So, whether you lean to the left politically (or just eat your matzah that way), may the vibrant remembrance of *yetzias Mitzrayim* continue to resonate within and inspire us to perceive Hashem and His kindliness and wisdom in more and more corners of the universe and more and more corners of our lives. For when we opt *not* to "ignore" Hashem—not even once—we will truly have made significant strides in acquiring the priceless blessing of true freedom.

Tazria

Speechless

Many years ago, I had the rare experience of davening *Minchah* in Congregation Ohaiv Shalom in Manhattan's Upper West Side. After *Aleinu*, several attendees recited the Mourner's Kaddish, among them a young man (he appeared to be in his late twenties) wearing blue jeans and sporting a baseball cap.

Now, one needs to be neither King Solomon nor Sherlock Holmes to realize that this particular fellow was unusually young to be saying Kaddish. In a (sincere) effort to convey some sort of impromptu empathy, I approached him outside of shul and struck up a casual conversation as we walked up the city block. "Nice to meet you. Are you from around here?" etc., etc. Having broken the ice, so to speak, I (respectfully) inquired for whom he was saying Kaddish. The young man responded that the Kaddish was for his father, who had recently passed away.

As we continued up the block together, he reciprocated the standard line of inquiries, "So, how about you…Are you from around here?"

"No," I responded, "I'm visiting from Monsey."

"So," he asked, "what brings you to the City?"

"My father's birthday," I mindlessly responded. Immediately sensing the crude insensitivity of that remark, I proceeded to seek out the nearest manhole to crawl into.

Of all the idiotic, out-to-lunch things to say?! I could have said I was in for a family get-together. Visiting my brother. Taking in Central Park.

Missing that Gotham mystique. A sale at Macy's. *Anything.* But my *"father's* birthday?!" Come on now.

How careful, sensitive, and deliberate must we be with our speech lest we offend, insult, antagonize, or negatively impact those with whom we are conversing.

And the person with tzaraas in whom there is the affliction, his garments shall be rent, the hair of his head shall go loose, and he must cover his head down to his lips...
Rashi: "Like a mourner."[53]

What is this notion of the afflicted person conducting himself "like a mourner"—a practice we don't find in conjunction with any other misconduct? A guy wears a *shaatnez* suit, does he act like a mourner? Ditto for someone who eats *treif.* So why is that such a fitting response for Mr. Tzaraas over here?

Perhaps the explanation stems from the fact that the root cause of *tzaraas* is often attributable to one's improper and harmful speech. Now, where in the universe of Torah practices and interpersonal relationships are we *most* attuned to speaking with deliberation? When we find ourselves in a shivah home, endeavoring to console a mourner:

- we refrain from speaking to the mourner until being spoken to;
- we wait to hear where s/he is coming from;
- we don't joke around;
- we don't engage in chitchat;
- the Yankees aren't the topic of discussion—nor is the NASDAQ.

We often leave the talking to others more adept at conveying sincere empathy with their words. If we have a vignette to share or a thought to express, we think it through (several times) before opening our mouths. Even then, our words invariably come across awkward and misplaced.

---

53   *Vayikra:* 13:45.

I have heard that the most "comforting" visits were often by those who had the least to say. On the flip side, it has also been noted that those who profess to "know *exactly* what you're going through" really didn't have the foggiest notion at all.

Thus, part and parcel of the *metzora*'s rehabilitation is the "training" he can glean from the deliberate, measured speech of the mourner's world. A milieu where silence is golden. An atmosphere where one's words are chosen with thoughtfulness. The realm where we take to heart the words of *Koheles*, "Be not rash with your mouth, and let not your heart be hasty to utter a word before Hashem…so let your words be few."[54]

May we merit to select our words in a means that will only brighten our world and the lives of others and not, G-d forbid, with the insensitivity that often (even inadvertently) can be so detrimental.

Measured words and deliberate speech are hallmarks of a Torah mind.

---

54   *Koheles* 5:1.

Metzora

At First Glance

Manhattan, June 9, 1994

The city was abuzz with Stanley Cup fever as the New York Rangers entered game five just one victory away from their first championship since the FDR Administration. With hopes of being "on-site" for the festivities, I commuted into NYC to watch the game amid a sea of enthusiastic Rangers fans at Champions Grill.

Alas, the Vancouver Canucks bested the Rangers that night by a score of 6-3. The celebratory champagne would remain on ice for several more nights (the Rangers wouldn't clinch victory until the seventh-game finale) and throngs of dejected fans turned in for the evening. Meanwhile, scores of reporters turned to the streets to interview crestfallen fans and get their take on the night's events.

Sure enough, as we were watching the post-game interviews, the analyst-reporter chimed in, "And now we're live from Champions with some Rangers fans..." My perplexed buddy looked at me and inquired, "Champions?! Aren't we *in* Champions!?" Sure enough, the very same interview that we were watching on the eighteen-inch screen above us was taking place real-time, in living color, right behind us, just a few yards away.

> *When you arrive in the land of Canaan that I give you as a*
> *possession, and I will place a tzaraas affliction upon a house in*
> *the land of your possession.*
>
> Rashi: *"This is a good tiding for them that afflictions come*
> *upon them because the Amorites hid treasures of gold in the*
> *walls of their houses all forty years that Israel was in the*
> *desert, and as a result of the affliction, he breaks down the*
> *house and finds them."*[55]

For those who found such an unexpected treasure (via this most unlikely of fashions), whatever disgruntled frustrations they harbored quickly gave way to relief and elation. Upon further review, it also served to reconfigure (or obliterate, as the case may be) any lingering self-delusions that we truly know what's best for ourselves. What we imagine to be beneficial could turn out anything but. What we lament as unfortunate can ultimately prove profitable and life-altering.

"Seeing," from the Torah's perspective, means much more than just the surface-level, visual perception of an event. Much more than the phenomenon that occurs when light rays hit the retina and are "magically" processed via the optic nerve. Yes, that type of sight may be decoded in your *brain*, but it does not mean that it has lodged in your *heart*. True, that may be considered "vision," but it does not yet amount to the Torah's notion of what it means to truly "see." When life is processed via the lenses of *emunah* and *bitachon*, "what you see" is rarely the sum total of "what you get."

Decades ago, psychologist Thomas Gordon introduced the world to the notion of "active listening." Along similar lines, the Torah offers a glimpse of what "active *seeing*" can accomplish. For starters, the desire to see "more than meets the eye" is a noble endeavor because it is a means of perceiving Hashem behind the scenes. Beyond that, one empowered with "active seeing" can (hopefully) shed

> When life is processed via the lenses of *emunah* and *bitachon*, "what you see" often pales in comparison to "what you get."

---

the apathy and disinterestedness that plagues so many of us as a result of the bombardment of information and imagery—good, bad and indifferent—the whole day through. As a noted neurologist told me, "In many instances, the cerebral work pad is full. We just can't process anymore." And thus, events that *should* strike an emotional chord within us go by the by and are unthinkingly discarded to some remote corner of our inbox.

The following story illustrates this idea. Rabbi Aryeh Levin, *zt"l*, was once standing outside his yeshiva in Jerusalem while the children were on a fifteen-minute recess break. His son, Chaim, a teacher in the yeshiva, was standing and observing, when suddenly his father turned to him. "What do you see, my son?" asked Reb Aryeh. "Why," his son answered, "children playing!"

"Tell me about them," said Reb Aryeh. "Well," answered Reb Chaim, "Dovid is standing near the door of the school, with his hands in his pockets, he probably is no athlete. Moishie is playing wildly, he probably is undisciplined. Yitzchak is analyzing how the clouds are drifting. I guess he was not counted in the game. But all in all, they are just a bunch of children playing."

Reb Aryeh turned to him and explained, "No, my son. You don't know how to watch the children. Dovid is near the door with his hands in his pockets because he has no sweater. His parents can't afford winter clothes for him. Moishie is wild because his *rebbi* scolded him and he is frustrated. And Yitzchak is moping because his mother is ill and he bears the responsibility to help with the entire household. In order to be a *rebbi*, you must know each boy's needs and make sure to give him the proper attention to fulfill those needs."

Life is happening all around us. We see what we want to see. When you want to see in two-dimensions, there are plenty of excuses to do so. Yet, when you strive to see the *whole* picture, the picture that Hashem wants us to see—that multidimensional, emotion-laden, psychologically rich, true vision of humanity—that is the moment when true connectivity is possible and, with it, the sensation that one is truly engaged in life. And not just a passive spectator.

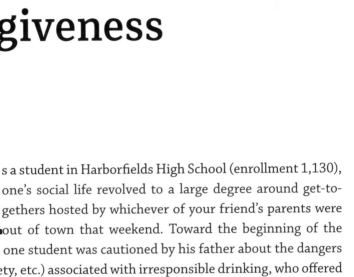

Acharei Mos

Beyond Forgiveness

As a student in Harborfields High School (enrollment 1,130), one's social life revolved to a large degree around get-to-gethers hosted by whichever of your friend's parents were out of town that weekend. Toward the beginning of the school year, one student was cautioned by his father about the dangers (health, safety, etc.) associated with irresponsible drinking, who offered a loving-yet-stern warning to his son to steer clear of such behavior. One Saturday night shortly thereafter, the son had succumbed to social pressures (as teens often do) and ran afoul of his father's wishes. Not only that, but upon returning home, the son must have done a lousy job of hiding his inebriated condition.

As you can imagine, Sunday morning was quite a scene. The son wasn't sure what he felt worse about—his grogginess or having disappointed his parents. The awkwardness of the moment was salvaged by one saving grace: the local pick-up—Sunday-morning touch football at the local Middle School. To the son's great relief (and disbelief), the father mustered the forgiveness and wherewithal to inquire, "Son, it's Sunday morning, aren't you coming to play?" The incredulous son was relieved to know that he hadn't been formally disowned. That was just the beginning—soon he would become privy to an episode that spoke volumes about a parent's undying love for his child and what lies at the outer bounds of forgiveness.

For those of you who know touch football, there's always that one hyper-revved-up guy, that fellow who's taking things just a little too seriously. (He's normally wearing a jersey of some sort, living out some pipe dream of playing in the NFL, and feeling the effects of his third highly caffeinated beverage.) Anyway, on this particular Sunday, Mr. Hyper was play after play taking out his machismo on the very same forlorn son mentioned above. Then, during one play, Mr. Hyper went over the line and roughed-up the son with his overly aggressive conduct. Without hesitation, the father picked up the ball, looked Mr. Hyper squarely in the face, and unflinchingly declared, "If you *ever* do that to *my son* again, I will break you in half!"

Well, as you can imagine, that was a game-changer. Mr. Hyper chilled out. No one started up with the son. The game proceeded without further fanfare. The participants went home. The son, however, would never be the same.

True, fathers' protection of their sons is part and parcel of the innate, paternal relationship...but that such an allegiance remained in place, notwithstanding the son's disobedience just the night before, spoke volumes as to the depth, permanence, and resiliency of a bond that is true and eternal.

> *For on this day He shall provide atonement for you to cleanse you; from all your sins before Hashem shall you be purified.*[56]

One of the most hopeful dimensions of Judaism can be found in the Divine notion of *teshuvah*, whereby the capacity to regret, return, and even undo one's misconduct is extended to virtually all Jews under a wide variety of circumstances. (In other words, like a loving parent, Hashem provides a very broad strike zone for the sincere penitent). In this respect, beseeching Hashem to accept (and facilitate) our *teshuvah* is not a once-a-year endeavor, but part of the fabric of our everyday *avodah* and *tefillah*.

---

56   *Vayikra* 16:30.

In this vein, Yom Kippur provides an opportunity to scale way beyond status quo ante, to accomplish much more than merely purging the spiritual "points" from our spiritual "license." Rather, it provides a rare and cherished capacity for *taharah*—for true purity—not just *despite* our miscues and imperfections, but *because* of those very blemishes and our resulting desire to come close to Hashem in their aftermath.

> *[Moshe] said, "Show me now Your glory.*[57]
>
> *Hashem passed before him and proclaimed: Hashem, Hashem, G-d, Compassionate and Gracious, Slow to Anger and Abundant in Kindness and Truth; Preserver of Kindness for thousands of generations, Forgiver of Iniquity…*[58]

Among the most potent *tefillos* in the arsenal of a sincere Jew's heart are the Thirteen Attributes of Mercy that Hashem revealed to Moshe Rabbeinu. They occupy a prominent role in the davening on national fast days, as well as during the Ten Days of Repentance. As one heads down the final stretch of Yom Kippur (about page eight hundred or so), hardly a page is turned without invoking these Thirteen Attributes in an eleventh-hour, last-ditch plea for Hashem to accept our *teshuvah*.

Thirteen Attributes of Mercy. Great. Fine. Wonderful. But don't you find the circumstances under which Hashem revealed these potent words a little bit odd? Maybe save them for right before Moshe's death. Maybe reveal them at Sinai along with the giving of the Torah. But right *after* Am Yisrael made its grievous error with the Golden Calf?! This hardly seems like the opportune time for Moshe to request a *greater* connection to Hashem and an unlikely time for Hashem to convey such an unprecedented revelation of His love for the Yidden.

It's like the accountant who, having made a colossal miscalculation resulting in the firm's loss of its most lucrative client, turning around and asking his boss for a raise. Nice idea. Bad timing.

---

57   *Shemos* 33:18.
58   Ibid. 34:6–7.

Not to take anything away from the deep, cosmic significance of this exchange between Hashem and Moshe, suffice to say (at least for this venue) that the post-*eigel* world created an environment that, while unexpected and lamentable, was ripe for *teshuvah* to an unparalleled degree. Precisely at the moment when Am Yisrael might have felt alienated and distant on account of their disobedience, the *Av Ha'rachamim* went out of His way, so to speak, to provide a glimpse into the vastness of His love for His Nation—a love that is unbreakable and resilient, long-suffering and patient.

The vast scope of Hashem's willingness to accept our sincere *teshuvah* testifies to the depths of His love for us.

Lawyers, doctors, Indian chiefs. Whatever we may be, we are all Hashem's children. The *Cheit Ha'eigel*, while clearly a low point in our nation's history—and one with cosmic repercussions—did, however, pave the way for a lesson in the nature of the inseverable bond we all keep with Hashem. More than merely providing us an effective spiritual "eraser," Hashem offered an opportunity for our forefathers—and a timeless lesson for us—that the heights of spirituality are still attainable, even from amid the depths of disobedience.

Kedoshim

Under the Influence

Two letters accompany me to shul every weekday. One is dated September 18, 1987, and reads: "Tomorrow you will be called to the Torah as a Bar Mitzvah. In answering that call, you will be forging yourself as the newest link in a chain that extends throughout the generations. You will receive from me a [tallis], as I received from my father, and he from his father, and his father from his father's father…It signifies morality and fairness, it signifies kindness and truth, and it signifies duty—a duty to live your life in a manner of which you and the Jewish people can be proud of." This is the letter I received from my father on the eve of my bar mitzvah.

The other is dated August 15, 1961 and reads: "Despite all this inhumane treatment, the Jewish religion and its teachings have been kept alive and vigorous by Jews who loved G-d and the Jewish religion, which is the most humane and ethical religion ever adopted by mankind…A true Jew lives a life in which every act committed must find grace in the eyes of G-d and mankind." This is the letter that my father received from *his* grandfather just a few months prior to my father's bar mitzvah. In this priceless correspondence, my great-grandfather expressed his sincere hopes that the approaching milestone would spark an "avid determination to take your place in the ranks of the good and true sons of David."

Every man shall revere his mother and his father...[59]

You shall rise in the presence of an old person and you shall honor the presence of an elder and you shall have fear of your G-d—I am Hashem[60]

As part of his Free Speech Movement in the 1960s, activist Jack Weinberg espoused the view that one should "not trust anyone over thirty." Even after the tumultuousness of the 1960s' counterculture has waned, society still champions the primacy of youth and often looks askance on the ways of the previous generation as old-fashioned and out of touch. Needless to say, the Torah's perspective is quite the contrary.

These were the sons of Levi in order of their birth: Gershon, Kehas, and Merari; the years of Levi's life were a hundred and thirty-seven years.[61]

Right smack in the Torah's dramatic narrative of Moshe's pleas to Pharaoh, Pharaoh's stubborn refusal to liberate Am Yisrael, and the crescendo leading up to the Ten Plagues, the Torah interrupts its description (seemingly without reason) to enumerate the lineage of Moshe and Aharon.

In the course of that discussion, *Seforno* offers an explanation why, of all the Tribes, *shevet Levi* produced all three leaders of Am Yisrael: Moshe, Aharon, and Miriam. Statistics would suggest that such positions of authority would be divided somewhat evenly among the sons of Yaakov. Why not one from *shevet Reuven*, one from *shevet Asher*, and so forth? What was unique about *shevet Levi* that facilitated the emergence of all three such leaders?

Seforno attributes this achievement to the fact that Levi outlived all his siblings. On account of that longevity, the younger generations possessed quantitatively more opportunities to be inspired and influenced

---

59   *Vayikra* 19:3.
60   Ibid. 19:32.
61   *Shemos* 6:16.

by their ancestors. The added interactions between Levi and his off-spring facilitated more wisdom, more understanding, more perception and, ultimately, a greater wherewithal for greatness in his descendants. This quantitatively and qualitatively greater capacity for *chochmah* and *binah* ultimately materialized in the triumvirate of leadership par excellence—Moshe, Aharon, and Miriam.

In our own lives, we have the opportunity to seek out influences that can propel us to greatness of character and to keener degrees of clarity. As my *rebbi*, Rav Moskovitz, would advise, "Wherever you are, sit next to the biggest *talmid chacham* in the room." Not just so you can sit and fire away question after question, but rather so you will gain a golden opportunity to observe his interactions with others, gauge his responses, and, ultimately, encounter a living example of what it means to be a mensch.

The *Orchos Tzaddikim*[62] reminds us that our hearts are like a blank journal and we possess the free will to choose what messages to engrave "on the tablet of your heart."[63] While we are bombarded with countless messages, sound bites and talking heads clamoring for our attention, such shallowness does not warrant being downloaded per se to the ledger of our souls. To the contrary, the wisehearted, discerning individual will seek out those living personifications of Torah, mitzvos, wisdom, and character that will enable their *neshamah* to shine forth, not just for themselves but, ultimately, for Am Yisrael.

> The wisehearted seek out opportunities to be influenced by those who possess the wisdom and character to facilitate their inner growth.

For only those who have been privy to such stellar influences have the opportunity—indeed the responsibility—to seek to influence others for the good and for the best.

---

62   Preface.

63   *Mishlei* 7:3.

Emor

All the King's Men

Notwithstanding its soothing sky-blue walls, the Kings County Clerk's Office is not for the faint of heart. The only ones who *really* know their way around the labyrinth of desks, windows, and amorphous cues are the "civil" servants whose personalities are often anything but civil. Quite the contrary, they all seemingly personify "Brooklyn bravado" to one degree or other. While in the midst of this vortex, you can't help but wonder

- how the pistol licenses keep separate from the marriage licenses;
- why, for some reason or other, the departments have not advanced technologically since the Reagan Administration.

Against this backdrop, you can appreciate the dilemma I faced when I ventured into the Clerk's Office on behalf of an employer to procure some official County document. The scene was chaos; picture your typical bureaucratic government office but slightly more savage. As I approached window #9, I realized there was only one fellow in front of me. In the absence of any formal line, I deliberately calculated the proper place to park myself—allotting enough space for the guy in front of me to conduct his business with some modicum of privacy, yet not allowing *too* much distance lest someone usurp my spot in line. Satisfied that I had struck the right balance, I put down my knapsack and began to rehearse my request.

100

Lo and behold, a customer who concluded his business at window #8 spun off of that adjacent line toward the archive room, only to trip right over my bag. While, fortunately, this gentleman managed to keep his balance (and his extensive paperwork), I found myself on the (unde-served) receiving end of a loud, obnoxious Brooklyn-ese "Hey, why don't you watch where you put your stuff?!" So much for my attempt to get out of Gotham unscathed. So much for my attempt to make a *kiddush Hashem*.

They shall be holy to their G-d and they shall not desecrate the Name of their G-d.[64]

The mission our forefathers accepted at Har Sinai transcended (mere-ly) the doing of mitzvos and desisting from *aveiros*. Beyond hanging *me-zuzos* and giving *tzedakah*, Am Yisrael was charged with the awesome re-sponsibility of serving as a "light unto the nations." Bearing this mantle places demands on every Yid, no matter the circumstances we find our-selves in, what mode of public transportation we find ourselves aboard, whomever we find ourselves interacting with. Be it nine to five or five to nine. Be it formal or informal. Be it completely anticipated or totally off-the-cuff.

Empowered by this awareness, we have the op-portunity—indeed, the privilege and the responsi-bility—to bring Godliness into that which is most mundane. Waiting in line at the bank, hoisting our luggage into the overhead racks, or navigating rush-hour traffic. Since the world at large is invariably watching, our capacity to demonstrate genuine *menschlichkeit* is, in turn, virtually unlimited. Forget ordination. Forget long black coats or long gray beards. If one is a Jew, one is a fully enlisted soldier in the King's army of "royal" guards. Day in and day out, we remain privileged to pursue righteousness, virtue, and purposefulness from the shul to the subway and every encounter along the way.

Encounters aren't mundane. To the contrary, they are a kiddush Hashem waiting to happen.

---

64 *Vayikra* 21:6.

Behar

Silence
and Praise

Negotiating the terms of the purchase and sale of a home is a common, humdrum occurrence and rarely provides material worthy of much thought. That being said, I was once privy to a particularly painful negotiation process between two couples (let's call them Mr. and Mrs. Buyer and Mr. and Mrs. Seller), which bears mention. As the parties discussed the various components of the deal, i.e., the purchase price, the down payment, the prospective closing date, and the conditions of sale, I was astonished to observe the following pattern unfold again and again.

While Mr. Seller and Mr. Buyer handled most of the brass tacks, dialoging between themselves, occasionally *Mrs.* Seller and *Mrs.* Buyer would offer their (usually emotionally based) comment or opinion. On multiple occasions, the well-intended comments of Mrs. Seller and Mrs. Buyer repeatedly weakened their respective bargaining tactics and cost themselves many thousands of dollars—a costly price tag simply for volunteering nonessential information that by all means should have been kept to themselves.

I felt like cringing. The husbands almost blew a gasket. "Just keep your mouth shut," was the overarching (albeit unspoken) sentiment, "and we'll all be much better off"—not to mention quite a bit wealthier. (Of course, in many other instances it is the men who should know better, so let's not assume this problem exists solely on one side of the gender "ledger.")

> *Do not harass one another, and you shall have fear of your G-d;*
> *for I am Hashem, your G-d.*
>
> *Rashi: "Here the Torah enjoins us regarding verbal harassment;*
> *that one should not oppress his fellow."[65]*

For any of us who have endured "blood-bubbling" encounters, we know what heroic measures of self-restraint are necessary to rein in our freedom of speech, which is poised to lash out with some stinging criticism or hurtful rebuke. At times like these, we need to tap into those inner reserves of discipline in order to stave off hurtful comments that, more often than not, are better left unsaid. One such episode of exemplary conduct can be found way back when, in, of all places, the Garden of Eden.

> *Hashem G-d took the man and placed him in the Garden of*
> *Eden...[66]*

Not bad. A picture-perfect day in Gan Eden—the garden of delights—with an eternity to bask in the peace and tranquility of G-d's pristine world. Before the sun set on that first day, however, Mrs. Adam (a.k.a. Chavah) offered a seemingly innocuous piece of advice (i.e., encouraging her husband to eat from the Tree of Knowledge) that managed not only to get them evicted from their blissful home in Gan Eden, but also brought death into the world and sentenced her husband to a life of toil (whether she burned the cholent or not, the Torah doesn't say). Wonderful. Off to a flying start. And for my next trick...

While many husbands would have blown their stack and commenced an onslaught of accusations and epithets toward their spouse, Adam

---

65   *Vayikra* 25:17.
66   *Bereishis* 2:15.

responds with unshaken equanimity and inestimable dignity. He doesn't throw dishes. He doesn't engage in name-calling. Rather, the Torah records how "the man called his wife's name Chavah because she had become the mother of all life."[67] *Precisely* at the very moment when he would seemingly be justified in focusing on her colossal miscue and flawed decision-making, he opted for the emotional high ground and focused on her unique and esteemed role as the "mother of all life."

Before lashing out at others, identify that which is positive, and focus on that which is praiseworthy.

When the sky seems to be falling and it appears obvious that it is someone *else's* fault, hearken to the path of Adam and muster whatever it takes to find positivity and purposefulness in your spouse, friend, teacher, student, employer, employee, landlord...whatever and whoever the case may be. A tall order indeed, but something that the human, created in G-d's image, is capable of accomplishing.

---

67   Ibid 3:20.

Bechukosai

Good to the Last Drop

The experience was quintessential Yerushalayim. That mesmerizing Yerushalayim Shabbos light emanating from the heavens. That invigorating Yerushalayim Shabbos breeze. That captivating sense of collegiality that engulfs Yidden of all walks and stripes—be it the *chassid* decked out in his *shtreimel* and Shabbos *bekeshe*, the IDF solider sporting his *kippah serugah*, the Sephardim, the Litvaks, and the tourists—who stroll the streets of Shaarei Chessed en route to their respective Shabbos meals. The streets are quiet(er). The shops are closed. The *kedushah* is palpable and ever-present. It's hard to imagine we were in Newark just forty-eight-hours earlier.

That twenty-minute walk from the Gra shul to our Yerushalayim apartment was, for me, as close to *sovei'a* (satiated) as I had ever known. When I arrived, my wife noted that the kids were having such a good time, did I mind waiting a bit to start the meal? Did I *mind*?! Not in the least. There was no desire to be anywhere else other than where I was. If the air-conditioning was a few degrees off, it mattered not in the least. If the soup wasn't piping hot, any disappointment paled in comparison to the overwhelming sense of satisfaction. As the saying goes, "We were playing with the house's money"—emotionally, psychologically, and spiritually. Any "imperfections" were muted by the embrace of Hashem's kindliness.

True, such moments are rare. But if you are fortunate enough to experience such a degree of satiation, it warrants a permanent place in your mind, heart, and psyche. One which you can revisit from time to time—especially when the current situation resembles a kaleidoscope of stressors, distractions, and hassles, each shoving satiation further and further beyond your orbit.

The land will give its fruit and you will eat to satisfaction.
Rashi: "One will feel satisfied despite having eaten a small quantity"[68]

You will eat your bread to satiety.
Rashi: "He will eat a bit and it will become blessed in his innards, i.e., it will be disproportionately satisfying."[69]

But if you will not listen to me…you will eat and not be sated.[70]
Rashi: "This is a curse inside the innards, i.e., which prevents the body from deriving satisfaction from food."[71]

As any restaurateur can attest, the quality of one's dining experience is multifaceted and owes as much to one's surroundings as to the meal itself (hence the ambiance of upscale eateries and hotels). The lighting. The music. The presentation. The clientele. The whole gestalt factors into the degree and extent of one's satisfaction (or lack thereof).

In this vein, is it possible we can significantly enhance our "satisfaction quotient" by processing our daily lives from a more macro, global perspective? For instance, you've finished supper, let's say noodles and sauce and some sliced tomatoes—the height of

---

68   *Vayikra* 25:19 Rashi based on *Mizrachi*.
69   Ibid. 26:5 Rashi based on Mizrachi.
70   Ibid. 26:26.
71   Ibid. Rashi.

gourmet—and you proceed to bless Hashem for the "nourishment and sustenance" you just consumed. Above and beyond the actual food itself, do I consider the fact that I enjoyed this meal with people whom I love (be it my spouse, family, or friends)? Does my *berachah* take into consideration that I could afford this meal? And afford to consume it in relative peacefulness and relative peace of mind? In my own home? With my own roof over my head? Without 1,001 allergies to contend with?

As the Torah attests, the blessing of satiation is not just a by-product of an *amount* of food, caloric intake, or even tastiness. Rather, the capacity to experience *true* satisfaction is a Divine blessing that transcends quantity. It beckons for one to consider the all-encompassing quality (tangible and intangible) of his or her reality and invite that good fortune into our hearts and minds.

> True "satiation" requires a heightened awareness of the full spectrum of blessings that envelops us.

As we broaden the scope of our awareness, as we become more attuned to the positive dimensions of our daily experiences—be it the people or the light or the breeze or the sights or the sounds—we'll find ourselves one step closer to the blessing of being truly *sovei'a*.

Bamidbar

The Power
of One

The notion of "feeling like a number" is a frequently uttered complaint of those struggling to find their stride in a community, school, job, etc., whose sheer size whittles away at their sense of self-worth and individuality. Taken to an extreme degree, the savage practices of the Nazis included branding Jews with numbers—all part of their systematic (albeit barbaric) attempts to dehumanize their captives and dismantle their spirits.

Along similar lines, we often find events of massive proportions difficult to internalize. Two hundred and eighty thousand deaths in the tsunami of 2004. Hundreds of thousands homeless after the Nepal earthquake in 2015. And that's nothing to say of truly staggering figures such as the twenty million lives that Stalin took during his merciless tyranny.

While I have not personally visited the United States Holocaust Museum in the nation's capital, it has been reported that one of the most emotional pivot points of the experience occurs when one is handed a passport of a particular Holocaust survivor. Apparently, the personal connectivity to one *specific* individual Holocaust survivor and their specific quest has a capacity to render history more "real." It facilitates a more acute emotional response than trying to wrap one's head around the sheer incomprehensibility of six million Jewish souls.

This phenomenon was apparent in Spielberg's production of the epic film *Schindler's List*. Amid the three-hour black-and-white cinematic tour de force, there were just a handful of images displayed in color, one of them being an innocent, pure young child in red walking amid the colorless nightmare. As one critic put it: "The use of color to follow the little girl in her red coat has by now achieved the stature of legendary." In part, because it served to provide a startling opportunity to personally connect—via one specific person—to a world (and an era), which, quite frankly, is emotionally and psychologically impenetrable to virtually anyone who did not experience such a nightmare.

In another vein, in summer 2014, the Shmira Project created a system whereby one could request the name of a *specific* IDF soldier to daven for. Thus, while all of us collectively davened for the safety and security of our brothers and sisters during Operation Protective Edge, somehow, the personal connection and emotional investment in one particular solider—be it Doron ben Ilana or Devorah bas Naomi—presented a heightened opportunity for one's prayers to find a more concrete and sincere expression.

Take a census of the entire assembly of the Children of Israel.[72]

Rashi: "Because of Yisrael's dearness before Hashem, He counts them at all times. When they departed from Egypt, He counted them. When they fell at the sin of the Golden Calf, He counted them. He counted them to determine the number of those who remained. And here, when He came to rest His Divine Presence upon them, He counted them."[73]

As the English name of *Sefer Bamidbar* (the Book of Numbers) attests, this particular section of the Torah focuses an awful lot on numbers.

---

72   *Bamidbar* 1:2.
73   Rashi to ibid. 1:1.

Numbers of this tribe and numbers of that tribe. Counting families. Counting firstborns.

Contrary to the dehumanizing notion of feeling "like a number," however, the Torah is renowned for the extreme value it places on each and every member of Am Yisrael.

Even the least learned of Jews are seemingly familiar with the profound wisdom that appears in the Gemara in *Sanhedrin*: "And whoever saves a single life, it is considered as if he saved an entire world."[74] A few sincere, contemplative minutes with this Chazal can revolutionize our attitude toward the greatness and pricelessness of every single Jew—regardless of their lineage, their wisdom, or their tax bracket.

While this message is always worthy of internalization, it is especially apropos as we approach the Divine treasure known as Shavuos, the Yom Tov on which we celebrate our receipt of Hashem's Torah and, beyond the Torah itself, the eternal relationship and unbreakable bond that was minted between Hashem and Am Yisrael at Har Sinai.

> Every single letter of the Torah is of immense importance...so too is every single Jew.

As we prepare ourselves to soar on these days—saturated with *kedushah* and commitment—may we be mindful that no Torah scroll is complete so long as even a single letter is missing...so too, our celebration of the Torah is not fully complete until we stand united, with *every* Jewish soul, ready, willing, and able to rededicate ourselves to Hashem amid boundless joy and unflinching determination.

---

74   37a.

Nasso

Truly Gifted

About ten years ago, my wife and I were tangentially involved in helping to make a *shidduch*. While we were not the primary *shadchanim*, an appreciative father-of-the-bride nevertheless sent us an extensive set of *sefarim* as an unnecessary (yet greatly appreciated) expression of gratitude. While I followed up with the traditional thank-you note that basic etiquette would mandate, I reckoned that a more sincere expression of thankfulness and appreciation would be as follows: Imagine when this gentleman would visit our home, he would see how well used those volumes were. Imagine he would see how their bindings were barely intact on account of all the intellectual "miles" logged therein. Imagine he could peruse the pages only to find extensive notes in the margin and a coffee stain here and there among the well-worn pages. Imagine every Rosh Chodesh he received a letter from me brimming with novel ideas I gleaned from his *sefarim*. Now, *that* would be an expression of gratitude far superior to the contents of any thank-you note I could muster. Indeed, from the vantage point of the gift giver, the knowledge that the recipient is utilizing that particular object—is enamored with it and gains so much practically from it—is likely to generate a deeper feeling of satisfaction than any note could possibly convey.

Along similar lines, as we leave the Shavuos period…what better way to celebrate than with our renewed zest for the Torah itself. Perhaps that's why *parashas Nasso* has 176 verses; it is the *longest* of all the *parashiyos* and is invariably read immediately on the heels of Shavuos.

Our enthusiastic learning of the Torah may very well be the greatest expression of our appreciation for such a Divine gift.

After all has been said and done over the last seven weeks plus—after the Haggadah and the four cups, the Afikomen and the cheesecake—as we say toward the end of *Ne'ilah* on Yom Kippur, "*Ein shiur rak haTorah ha'zos*—there is nothing remaining except for this Torah." It was, and remains, our unique national heritage. It was, and remains, our national lifeline to the past and link to the future. Our enthusiastic rededication to our *limud haTorah* may very well be the most apt expression of our gratitude. More time. More focus. More dedication. More excitement. Renewed ambitions. With a re-piqued enthusiasm for the Torah and a rekindled desire to internalize its timeless *chochmah*, may the days that come…between now and Sukkos…truly be a time of joyfulness, a *zman simchah*, for Yidden everywhere.[75]

---

75   Bartinura, *Bikkurim* 1:6.

Behaalosecha

Age-Old Wisdom

Having secured admission to the Boston College Law School in the winter of my senior year, I turned my sights to what I *really* wanted to do. Teaching literature in a New England private school. Sports writing for an out-of-town newspaper. Politics on Capitol Hill. As winter gave way to spring, those more "glorious" dreams evaporated in the winds of reality check, and law school emerged as the clear (and only) viable post-college option for an English major such as myself. But Boston College?! My ego repeatedly advised me that I "deserved" to attend a top-tier law school (NYU, Penn, or Georgetown). Apparently, their respective admissions' offices didn't seem to think so. As a result, I languished on a host of waiting lists beyond graduation and throughout the summer, hoping that a different (i.e., better) option would come to fruition.

My frustration with the "situation" underwent a radical transformation, however, when my grandfather, of blessed memory, called one midsummer's night. [By way of context, I shared a meaningful relationship with my Grandy, who often prided himself on being "my toughest critic."]

"How are you doing?" he inquired.

"OK, I suppose."

"Just OK?" he asked. "What's troubling you?"

"Well," I sheepishly confessed, "it seems like I'm headed to BC for law school and, well, I always imagined I'd go to a better school."

"Jared," he said with that dramatic, grandfatherly pause, "that's a lousy attitude. Tell me," he probed, "is there a roof over your head? Does anything hurt you? Do your parents love you? Well, then…you're a very blessed young man." With the perspective of one who lived through the Depression and the sagacity of an octogenarian, he added, "Trust me. You're going to get to a point in life where no one will ask—let alone care—where you went to law school."

Gather for me seventy men from the elders of Yisrael…and they shall bear the burden of the people with you [i.e., Moshe].[76]

The Torah relates how Am Yisrael leveled a series of unwarranted complaints against Hashem—notwithstanding the fact that they were privy firsthand to Hashem's immense kindliness and protection during their travels through the Wilderness. Their basic physical needs (food, drink, shelter, clothing) were miraculously provided for in a manner that required only minimal exertion. Spiritually speaking, they continued to merit a close proximity to Hashem and relished the opportunity to learn from no less than Moshe Rabbeinu. Given such circumstances, how could these complaints have taken root, and, further, why was the appointment of seventy elders the appropriate countermeasure to thwart future grumblings and protests?

In a truly stellar essay, "The Test of the Manna and Bread" (required reading, for sure), Rav Avigdor Miller, *zt"l*, offers a systematic diagnosis of the core problem and a precise analysis of the Torah's antidote.[77] While I cannot do justice to such a masterpiece of profundity and practicality, the idea posited is as follows:

---

76   *Bamidbar* 11:16–17.
77   *Shaarei Orah* (vol. I, ch. 16).

Complaints, Rav Miller explains, take root in a mind (or heart) that has forgotten Hashem and His boundless kindliness that permeates every nook of our lives and every second of our day. Life itself. Health (mental and physical). Family. Sustenance. Peace. And innumerable other examples.

One who is mindful of these blessings will invariably know deep-seated satisfaction and happiness. One for whom such gifts fail to register, however, is bound to feel dissatisfied and will vocalize such dissatisfaction in the form of protest and critique.

> Complaints emerge from a mind and heart that has forgotten the boundless kindliness that Hashem bestows upon us constantly.

Against this backdrop, the role of the seventy elders was specifically to reorient Am Yisrael to those abundant blessings that were *already* present in their lives. To re-emphasize the basics that should be the catalyst for heartfelt praise while de-emphasizing the "nonessentials" that gave rise to unwarranted kvetching.

The elders—imbued with the wisdom and appreciation of life experience—were uniquely suited to teach the younger generation(s) of Jews the *true* measure of their wealth, the concomitant opportunity to recognize Hashem's largesse, and the associated obligation to serve Hashem out of deep-seated joy and appreciation.

True, there is no shortage of things to complain about—the humid weather, New Jersey traffic, the cost of living, New York airports, et al. Yet for those such as ourselves, who are privileged to learn from our elders; who are fortunate enough to incorporate their sound evaluation of what's truly important; who have the opportunity to readjust our lenses so that we can view life through the prism of *their* wisdom, any would-be complaints are understandably muted when assessed in light of the undeserved, overwhelming, and underappreciated blessings that we all are constantly receiving from Hashem.

Shelach

Spies Like Us

reat museums inevitably possess a "signature" masterpiece that stands out above and beyond the other works in their collection. For instance, The Louvre (Paris) attracts some six million visitors annually—and I venture to say that few (if any) leave before viewing Da Vinci's *Mona Lisa* (arguably the world's most famous painting). Closer to home, Van Gogh's *The Starry Night* is the "highlight" work of the 3,600 paintings and sculptures on display in Manhattan's Museum of Modern Art.

Thus, as I worked my way through the two thousand Dutch paintings (a lot of windmills, I recall) in Amsterdam's world-famous Rijksmuseum, they were all somewhat of a lead-up to the gallery's pièce-de-résistance: Rembrandt's classic *Night Watch*. Finally, toward the very end of the museum, I finally encountered the legendary work.

True, I would admit, it was impressive. The colors. The light and shadowing. The expressiveness of the characters depicted therein. Nevertheless, I was somewhat disappointed in at least two respects:

- First, the work was about the size of a placemat—much smaller than I had anticipated.
- Second, why were so many fellow tourists strolling right along without stopping to gaze and appreciate this monumental artistic work?! Oh well, must be these folks didn't possess the sophisticated "eye" for art appreciation that I could (seemingly) boast of.

116

After a few minutes of observation, I turned the corner only to find...the real *Night Watch* displayed prominently in the next room. It was colossal in size (nearly 12 feet by 14 feet). It was surrounded by tourists, Danes, and budding artisans basking in this amazing feat of human artistic expression. Turns out that the "postcard" I had originally mistaken as the real *Night Watch* was some sort of lithograph designed to show what the painting had looked like prior to certain alterations that were undertaken in order to transport the national treasure to its current location. As for me, apparently my artistic know-how wasn't *quite* as sophisticated after all. I casually found a seat, hoping that no one had noticed my gaffe and proceeded to don my best "I knew that" countenance.

Not everything is what it appears to be. What masquerades as reality is often just a façade, whereas that which is truly genuine and precious frequently goes overlooked.

Why was the passage of the spies placed next to the passage of Miriam? For she was stricken over matters of speech...and these [spies] saw and yet did not take a lesson from her.[78]

At first glance, the connection between the episode of Miriam and the tragic episode of the spies is readily apparent, i.e., both failed to adhere to the laws of *shemiras ha'lashon*, which prohibit derogatory speech, and both suffered serious consequences as a result.

- Miriam spoke negatively about her brother Moshe.
- The spies offered a slanderous report about Eretz Yisrael.

A relatively straightforward equation.

In a different vein, the *Mashgiach*, Rabbi Ben Tzion Kokis, suggested there is another lesson that the spies could have (and should have) gleaned from Miriam—a fundamental notion in how we perceive

---

78   Rashi, *Bamidbar* 13:2.

reality and make value judgments based on that perception. Had the spies taken *this* lesson to heart, perhaps the catastrophic results of their mission could have been mitigated or avoided altogether.

Let's revisit Miriam's assessment of Moshe's decision to remain separate from his wife. From Miriam's perspective, this scenario seemed to be a carbon copy of circumstances that existed decades ago in Mitzrayim. Facing the cruel reality of Pharaoh's heartless decrees, her father Amram decreed that Jewish spouses should separate from one another. Miriam perceived the shortsightedness of that decision and boldly intervened. Specifically, Miriam pointed out that Amram's decree would essentially ensure that neither Jewish males *nor females* would be born and hence was actually crueler and more encompassing than Pharaoh's heartless legislation. As a result of Miriam's assessment of the scenario and proactive involvement, her parents remarried and Moshe Rabbeinu was born of that union, thereby setting the wheels of the redemption from Mitzrayim into motion.

Fast-forward a bit and Miriam (again) observes a leader of Am Yisrael (this time Moshe) separate from his wife. *Hey,* she reflects, *this fact pattern looks awfully familiar to what played itself out years ago.* She recalls how she intervened back then and how her willingness to do so essentially saved the Jewish People. Faced with a *seemingly* identical situation, Miriam (again) offers a proactive critique of that conduct. Yet, lo and behold, as we learned last week, her assessment (this time around) was erroneous and her decision to meddle with the matter was ill-advised.

Turning to the spies, even if everything they said they saw was accurate, i.e., that the inhabitants of the land were mighty, that their cities were fortified to the hilt, that the land *did* devour its inhabitants, the spies, nevertheless, failed to account for the fact that one's own perception of their so-called reality can be flawed. It can be subject to biases (conscious or subconscious) and thus is not necessarily the sole yardstick upon which to base weighty decisions. Had the spies merely reported what they saw, *without* drawing the conclusion that entering Eretz Yisrael was a lost cause, who knows what consequences could have been avoided? Had they offered their reconnaissance report *without* opining that the entire destiny of the Jewish People was doomed to fail, perhaps we would be honoring their valiant conduct on behalf of their nation rather than second-guessing them for eternity.

The lesson from Miriam (and now the lesson from the spies) is that total reliance upon one's perception of reality—no matter how sure one is of their *own* perception—remains a risky proposition. Indeed, one is rarely (if ever) capable of true objectivity, and the acquisition of true *daas Torah* frequently (if not always) calls for the input of an outsider, whose wisdom, sagacity, and equanimity can facilitate a true perception of the true reality.

> Total reliance on one's own perception of reality is a risky proposition.

Korach

Divided
We Fall

I n the fall of 2000, each member of the Supreme Judicial Court's fresh crop of law clerks was eager to hit the ground running. Working for the Commonwealth of Massachusetts's highest court was a rare and sought-after opportunity to acquire a behind-the-scenes view of the process whereby high-profile cases were debated and decided; where matters of first impression were deliberated upon; where opinions that would become binding precedent on the Commonwealth were inked; and where (hopefully) justice was safeguarded and administered.

For many of my fresh-out-of-law-school colleagues, it was also an opportunity to showcase one's legal acumen and flair for research and writing, and (potentially) serve as a stepping-stone to an enriching and successful career in the legal/judicial profession.

That being said, from the outset, it became readily apparent that the clerks' toil would be an odyssey of anonymity. Our hours and efforts and drafts and re-drafts would never bear our name (at least not to anyone outside of chambers). Rather, one name—and one name only—would appear on each opinion, that being Justice Ireland (our boss), and our collective job was to pool our time, talents, and experience toward achieving one singular goal: to make sure that *his* opinions were as clear, fair, well-reasoned, erudite, and unassailable as possible.

Needless to say, in order to accomplish this end, personal drives for recognition and accomplishment invariably gave way to the greater good of "chambers." Personal milestones and the limelight would necessarily have to wait if we aspired to discharge our responsibilities to "His Honor" and the Commonwealth.

Was it rewarding? Absolutely. Is our name or legacy recorded anywhere? Absolutely not.

Moshe said to Aharon, "Take the firepan and put on it fire from the Altar and place incense—and take it quickly to the assembly and provide atonement for them...",[79]

Why, of all things, was the *ketores*—incense mixture—the spiritual antidote to quell Korach's insurrection?

Our impression of Korach, the Torah's quintessential "rebel with a cause," is one whose personal shortcomings spurred him to disassociate himself from the collective lifeblood of Am Yisrael. In order to foment his radical (and heretical) political views, he needed to "separate from the rest of the assembly."[80] His contentiousness (while cloaked in a thin veil of egalitarianism) ultimately emanated from jealousy and sour grapes over the fact that he *personally* had been overlooked for an office of distinction among the *Levi'im*.

If you have ever been privy to *machlokes* (either personally, as a bystander, or as a peacemaker) you can attest to the fact that disputes are inevitably the consequence of "too many egos" seeking "too many disparate agendas." In contrast, when humbler souls are willing to subjugate their personal views for the greater good of the group, one (often) finds unity and accord as opposed to divisiveness and discord.

Machlokes is often the by-product of "too many egos" seeking "too many disparate agendas."

---

79   *Bamidbar* 17:11.
80   Ibid. 16:1.

Korach's egotistical self-centeredness presented a formidable threat to the unity of Am Yisrael. In this respect, perhaps that is precisely why the *ketores* proved to be the appropriate countermeasure to quash the rebellion. For, as the Talmud teaches,[81] one of the essential ingredients in the *ketores* concoction is a spice known as *galbanum*, which possessed a distinctively foul aroma. Nevertheless, this unpleasant element was deliberately *included* in the Divine *ketores* recipe to hammer home the notion that *every* Jew—even those who have strayed far from the path of observance—should be included in the communal davening.[82] We are not truly one unless everyone is truly among us. At the end of the day, whatever you call it, factionalism and divisiveness are antithetical to our national, collective destiny. This being the case, the insidiousness of Korach's selfishness that threatened to splinter the nation was quelled *specifically* by the *ketores*, which represents the epitome of Jewish *inclusiveness*.

With this in mind, may the drives for personal glory-seeking and one-upmanship yield to the needs of the greater good of Am Yisrael and our respective communities. May we achieve the oneness the *ketores* represents and thereby realize the vision of one united Beis Yisrael.

---

81   *Kerisos* 6b.
82   Rashi, *Shemos* 30:34.

Chukas

Roadside Support

In addition to his Rabbinic post in Cincinnati, Rabbi Eliezer Silver, *zt"l*, worked tirelessly to save thousands of Jewish lives during World War II. As president of the Vaad Hatzalah (Rescue Committee), he spearheaded initiative after initiative in the desperate hope of rescuing his Jewish brethren trapped in war-torn Europe. Be it fund-raising (to the tune of $5 million—approximately $65 million in today's economy) or galvanizing domestic political pressure; be it securing emergency visas or his legendary efforts to save Jewish children who had been taken in by French monasteries during the Holocaust—*neshamos* were at stake and, hence, no effort could be spared.

The story is told of how a survivor of the concentration camps ultimately emigrated to America and found his way to Cincinnati. While this gentleman had kept Torah and mitzvos in his youth, the atrocities of the war (through which he lost virtually all of his family and loved ones) had broken his belief in Hashem and morality. His interest in observance and mitzvos was snuffed out amid the pain and trauma. Far be it for us to judge such extreme tests of faith. Suffice to say that some members of Cincinnati's Orthodox community encouraged this fellow to meet with Rabbi Silver in the hopes that some consolation and meaningfulness could be salvaged.

At this fateful meeting, as the story goes, the parties exchanged pleasantries. At some point in the conversation, this emotionally broken yet defiant individual declared, "Rabbi! Hashem took the good ones [to heaven] and left the *pesoles* (i.e., the inferior ones) to live." Feeling this fellow Yid's pain to his core, Rabbi Silver embraced him, began to weep and said only, "You're right. You're right." They hugged one another and cried together for who knows how long.

Rabbi Silver offered no sophisticated discussions about how those lost ones were somehow, someway, better off in the Next World. No "defense" of Hashem's Divine Master Plan (that often escapes our comprehension). No "everything has a reason, we just don't know it." No pep talk in *emunah* or *bitachon*. No "I know exactly what you're going through." Just a sincere attempt to meet a heartbroken Jew where his emotional rubber met his emotional road.

The postscript is that they developed a deep-seated respect for one another and sincere friendship. It is reported that Rabbi Silver ultimately inspired this man to re-embrace his heritage and resume his keeping of mitzvos. Years later, they recounted their initial meeting, whereby the man reminisced, "Rabbi, had you responded in *any other way*, I would have said goodbye and walked away."

They journeyed from Mount Hor by way of the Sea of Reeds to go around the land of Edom, and the spirit of the people grew short with the road.[83]
Rashi: *"The hardship of the road…became difficult for them."*[84]

Anyone who's traveled for an extended period of time can relate to the rigors of the road. Living out of a suitcase is no fun, and take-out food becomes tiresome. But, hey, the Jews were seasoned desert voyagers by this point. They still had their faithful shepherd Moshe and still

---

83   *Bamidbar* 21:4.
84   Ibid.

merited water and nourishment via Divine channels. Why all of a sudden did they "speak up against Hashem and Moshe [kvetching], 'Why have you brought us up from Egypt to die in this wilderness? For...our soul is at its limit with the insubstantial food (i.e., the *mahn*)."[85]

Perhaps this outburst and the emotional state that gave rise to it can be traced to the death of the beloved Aharon HaKohen (just a few lines earlier). As the Mishnah in *Pirkei Avos*[86] attests, the calling card of Aharon HaKohen was his love and dedication to the emotional well-being of his fellow Yidden. He was known throughout Am Yisrael as one who "would pursue peace and instill love between parties to a quarrel and between a man and his wife."[87] Notwithstanding his role as the *Kohen Gadol*, the lofty stature associated with being the Jewish Nation's second-in-command, and the communal obligations he shouldered, Aharon HaKohen never lost sight of the *individual* and his or her particular plight.

Returning to Am Yisrael's frustration with the "hardship of the road," Rashi offers the following emotionally spot-on diagnosis: "The expression 'shortening of spirit' applies to anything that is difficult to a person, like a person upon whom something disturbing falls, and this state of mind is not broad enough to accept that thing, and he does not have room within his heart where the pain might abide."[88]

Perhaps, throughout all these years of desert wandering, Am Yisrael suffered similar "hardships," and yet those difficulties were bearable precisely *because* of Aharon HaKohen's presence and his unique capacity to mend that emotional breach in the heart of his fellow Jew. Now, however, in the post-Aharon era, no one was as equipped to provide the emotional bandwidth necessary, day in and day out, to help endure such trials and tribulations. In short, the "hardship of the road" was felt more acutely now that Aharon was not available to provide *chizuk* and support.

---

85   Ibid. 21:5–6.
86   *Avos* 1:12.
87   *Bamidbar*, Rashi 20:29.
88   Ibid. 21:4.

In our own lives, I venture to say one need not look far to find someone whose "state of mind is not broad enough to accept" hardship or who "does not have room within his heart where the pain might abide."

You can provide those emotional shoulders for someone to lean on.

You can be those listening ears for a troubled soul to voice their pain.

You can walk in the shoes of Aharon HaKohen and provide the psychological scaffolding to enable a Jew to keep on trucking despite the static of self-doubt urging them to throw in the towel.

Forget about dissertations and sermons. Torpedo the deep philosophical justifications, and banish the clichés for some other time. Reconfigure the architecture of your own heart in order to provide the "room" that your fellow lacks in his own heart.

With sincerity, you can be the one to mitigate their loneliness.

With patience, you can help them right the ship.

With heartfelt validation, who knows how much life you can breathe into another's emotional sails. And in so doing, you will have carried the torch of Rabbi Eliezer Silver, whose dedication and understanding bore the hallmarks of Aharon HaKohen, who brought all of us closer to Torah. How? Not with *derashahs* and scholarship. Not with sermons and theology. But rather with his undying love of *shalom*, his selfless pursuit of *shalom*, and his unwavering love of his fellow.

Balak

Present Tents

Noted conservative author and commentator, William F. Buckley, Jr., was greatly enamored of sailing and often wrote about the centrality of that pastime in forming his outlook on life. At one point he sailed a boat that carried the name *Querencia*. The word "querencia," it seems, refers to an unusual phenomenon found in the hot and dusty commotion of a Spanish bullfighting ring. Apparently, no matter how chaotic Mr. Bull's life would get—dealing with Señor Matador's prodding and taunting; coping with the cheers and jeers of throngs of rowdy sombrero-wearing spectators—there was always one place in the ring that Mr. Bull would feel completely at ease. An innate, inner calm amid the swirling storm. A tangible serenity despite an increasingly hostile environment. A place to escape and regroup.

By all accounts, the wicked prophet Bilaam ranks high on the list of Am Yisrael's archenemies. His diabolical scheme to facilitate immoral conduct between Jewish men and Moabite and Midianite women was ultimately responsible for the loss of twenty-four thousand Jewish lives. Given Bilaam's disdainfulness, I find it unusual how frequently his "praise" of Klal Yisrael appears in the course of our davening.

Every year, we encounter Bilaam in our Rosh Hashanah *Mussaf*: "Hashem…is with him [i.e., Yaakov], and the friendship of the King is in him."[89] We find the Sages seriously considered uploading Bilaam's words directly into, of all places, the daily reading of *Shema* (ultimately opted against on account of its lengthiness). And perhaps, most famously, the words that so many of us utter as we step over the threshold into shul each morning:

> *How goodly are your tents, O Jacob; your dwelling places, O Israel.*[90]

The Talmud[91] explains that these tents and dwelling places actually refer to our *shuls* and *batei midrash*. Moreover, the Gemara explains that these bastions of spirituality and communal connectivity would endure throughout the long and bitter exile.

Who doesn't feel an innate sense of camaraderie upon walking into a shul (if you don't, maybe it's time to consider changing shuls or, at least, changing your mindset). I recall being in the French Riviera (a town called Nice, which actually was rather nice) and spending Yom Kippur with French Yidden, with whom I shared no common language and no common culture. Needless to say, we did share *Kol Nidrei* in common. Our Shema was identical. And the reading of Yonah was completely in sync. We could barely communicate and yet I felt completely at home. Ditto for shuls from La Jolla to Raleigh to Florence. A universal home away from home.

With life spinning at an ever-increasing pitch, the opportunities for inward serenity are more and more necessary, yet harder and harder to come by. In order to reboot, reset, and reengage life from a vantage point of balance and resourcefulness, it behooves each and every one of us to find that particular space and place that can serve as our personal querencia.

And you need not seek your querencia in a bullring (or a yacht). Rather, for many of us, a shul, yeshiva, or *beis midrash* possesses a

---

89   *Bamidbar* 23:21.
90   Ibid. 24:5.
91   *Sanhedrin* 105.

unique, somewhat inexplicable capacity to generate peacefulness and *menuchas ha'nefesh*. Grounding.

There is a certain shul that occupies such a special place in my life. It is two hundred miles away. I visit once a year (if that). And yet it is always available—mentally, at least—to retreat to and find *menuchah*, quietude, and realignment. Between you and me (don't tell anyone), just listening to the shul's answering machine, "We have a daily morning minyan at 6:30 and 7:30…" propels me to a place of clarity, confidence, and conviction to reengage life's challenges. The light of the shul. The Rav. The dedicated and earnest souls who pour out their hearts to Hashem and dedicate their lives to one another. It's priceless. It's personal. It's often indescribable. And it's essential.

Such is the Eternal promise that Hashem conveyed via a most unlikely spokesperson, Bilaam. Our shuls are treasures. They light up the night of exile like a lighthouse beaconing rays of hope to storm-tossed shipmen seeking a harbor in the tempest. Seek and ye shall find a place of *menuchah* amid these soul-restoring tents and dwelling places. The chandeliers are optional. The marble floors are merely a bonus. Some shuls are makeshift. Some are grandiose. Some are teeming with new members. Some are a faint echo of what they were in yesteryear.

With the world spinning at a dizzying pace, our shuls can provide the serenity and recalibration that are so desperately needed and yet in such short supply.

But they boast at least one thing in common: the opportunity to meet Hashem, to regain clarity, and to emerge inspired to meet the challenges of life. See, once again, "how goodly" are those tents and what awaits those who are savvy enough to capitalize upon these "tents" of clarity.

Pinchas

Spanning the Generation Gap

A s a young adult, I had the opportunity to embark upon various voyages to various parts of the world (some of which you are familiar with by now). As a family ritual of sorts, I would invariably receive a letter from my grandfather a few days in advance of my trip. True to form, the letter was brief, to the point, and a unique blend of new-school love and old-school honor.

Grandy's pre-vacation letters usually included a twenty-dollar bill along with the following hand-written sentiments (more or less): *Dear Jared, I hope you have a wonderful trip. Enjoy, and remember not to do anything that will tarnish the family name. Love, Grandy*

Tarnish the family name?! Uh, who are we—the Rockefellers? The Carnegies? The Kennedys? Who said we had a family name and why was it so essential to keep it squeaky clean…?

Because the tribes were humiliating Pinchas...this is why the Torah comes and traces his ancestry to Aharon.[92]

In places where the Torah traces the ancestry of a tzaddik [i.e., the righteous Pinchas] for praise, it gives the ancestry of the wicked [Zimri] for disparagement.[93]

The daughters of Tzelaphchad, son of Hepher, son of Gilead, son of Machir, son of Menasheh...son of Yosef.[94]

Rashi: This lineage is listed "to teach you that they were all righteous..." and thus, "traces this ancestry to their credit."

Why is the Torah so preoccupied with lineages? Since when did Hashem become so interested in genealogy? The events of *parashas Pinchas* are incredibly important in and of themselves in terms of our nation's survival in the Wilderness and in conjunction with the ultimate apportionment of Eretz Yisrael. Do we really have to freeze-frame on every hero and heroine and double-click five generations earlier?

Be it Pinchas's courage in slaying Zimri and Kozbi or Tzelaphchad's daughters' heartfelt yearning for Eretz Yisrael, the Torah reminds us that our actions (and their consequences) are not to be viewed in isolation. Nor are they to be considered even in the context of a particular era and locale. Rather, one's conduct has moral repercussions for the world at large, and ethical reverberations for generations to come. In this respect, we are living not just in and of ourselves, but rather riding the momentum from our ancestors' dedication, while helping to set the tone for our descendants' continued commitment to Torah and Yiddishkeit.

Closer to home, my family and I reap the spiritual dividends of Jennie (Schprintzy) Viders' decision to steadfastly adhere to the principles of *tzniyus* (modesty), notwithstanding the challenges that awaited

---

92   Rashi, *Bamidbar* 25:11.
93   Ibid. 25:14.
94   *Bamidbar* 27:1.

her arrival in the new (and foreign) world of secular America in 1886. Ditto for Rabbi Avraham Eliyahu Kitov (Mokotovsky), who diligently maintained his Torah studies despite a life of wearying physical labor in 1920s Warsaw. When these giants of yesteryear were able to withstand the physical and spiritual challenges of their particular time and place, their respective self-sacrifices simultaneously planted the seeds for spirituality and truth-seeking that would come to fruition generations down the line.

Marching forward in time as well, that extra effort that *we* can muster in our own performance of mitzvos and *avodas Hashem* generates a reservoir of merits for our own descendants—in (perhaps) foreign shores and amid (perhaps) radically different societies—to live up to the specific challenges that *they* will face.

Since we inevitably confront incessant obstacles to sincere growth—be it the allure of inertia; the vulnerability associated with adopting sincere change; the spiritual and emotional malaise that finds a way to dampen or spirits—the knowledge that we are living not *only* for today but also for generations hence can serve as a gateway to access inner potential and an impetus to push through the inertia. After all, it's not just *my* Judaism at stake…it could very well impact some great-great-grand-nephew way on down the line.

> The powerful play goes on and you may contribute a verse—what meaningful and inspiring legacy will you leave for the generations to come?

Enlightened (and empowered) by the Torah's emphasis on lineage, ancestry, and multigenerational merits, we can be *mekadesh* the words of the poet Walt Whitman who inquired, "What good amid these, O me, O life?" to which he answered, "That you are here—that life exists and identity / That the powerful play goes on, and you may contribute a verse."

So too, our lives and those of Yidden in every place and at all times. We live with the opportunity and obligation to contribute a verse of dedication, positivity, and observance that will echo into eternity. What will *your* verse be?

Mattos

Full Faith and Credit

With Shabbos just a few hours away, my wife called to inquire: "Hi. How are you? So...what's your timing look like?" I had a hunch that this was the prelude to a request for just "one last" pre-Shabbos errand. This weekly rite of passage for Jewish husbands the world over is invariably followed by the words, "Can I trouble you to..." or "Are you anywhere near..."

This particular Friday, though, was no sugar-coated request. "You're not going to be thrilled about this..." my wife opined (and she was right). "We need food for the chickens. [Yes, there was a time we raised chickens; it didn't turn out well for the poultry population, but that's another story for another time.] They have it at the pet store on Route 59 in Nanuet."

(Now for those of you who haven't merited the pleasure of traveling Route 59 on *erev Shabbos*, it's a true gauge of the effectiveness of one's brakes—and patience—and lends a new definition to "stop-and-go." Sort of like a *frum* version of rush hour on the Northern Boulevard, for those of you who can appreciate Long Island traffic.)

"Well," I responded, knowing that my trip to the pet store was a fait accompli, "I still have to get some documents xeroxed, then arrange to ship them overnight, make a deposit at First Niagara Bank, and a withdrawal from Chase bank." On the face of things, this lineup did not appear to be a recipe for that long-awaited, chilled-out *erev Shabbos*.

Yet just when it looked like this *erev Shabbos* was going down to the wire, I meandered down Route 59 only to discover (and I kid you not):

- PetSmart at 155 East Route 59;
- Chase Bank at 123 East Route 59;
- First Niagara at 117 East Route 59; and
- FedEx/Kinko's at 111 East Route 59!

All four destinations are virtually adjacent to one another. One parking lot. Copies copied. Documents overnighted. Deposit deposited. Withdrawal in hand. Chicken food (to go)…and, as they say at Staples, "That was easy."

> *Go and proclaim in the ears of Jerusalem, saying, "Thus said Hashem: I remember for your sake the kindness of your youth, the love of your bridal days, your following after Me in the Wilderness, in a land not sown."*[95]

Besides being one of the most well-known expressions of Hashem's love for Am Yisrael, the Alter from Kelm amplifies this verse's sentiments by highlighting several contextual points. First, the *navi* is not speaking to the generation that *actually* "followed after Hashem in the Wilderness, in a land not sown." To the contrary, he is addressing the distant descendants of the storied generation that left Mitzrayim. Second, this sentimental recollection of Am Yisrael happens to fall out right smack in the middle of a scathing rebuke of their misconduct, i.e., of "forsaking" Hashem.[96] Third, Hashem seems to build up the magnitude of the event, i.e., following Hashem blindly into the Wilderness. After all, Hashem did systematically dismantle Mitzrayim with plagues

---

95   *Yirmiyahu 2:2, Haftaras Mattos.*
96   Ibid. 1:16.

and wonders—was there a legitimate reason *not* to follow Him further?

Nevertheless, this vignette highlights the fact that Hashem goes "out of His way," so to speak, to hold on to this pristine moment of our nation's demonstration of *emunah* and *bitachon*. Even if it was generations earlier. Even if it was not necessarily the biggest leap of faith. And even if now they had veered far from that level of trust. In this respect, we can follow in Hashem's ways and endeavor to commemorate and collate such watershed moments of *emunah* and *bitachon* from our own lives. More than that, we can perpetually visit and revisit those instances where Hashem made a clear cameo appearance in our daily lives, thereby creating a personal reservoir of *emunah*, *bitachon*, and *chizuk* to be gleaned therefrom.

True, the sea didn't split for me that day on Route 59. Nor did the chicken feed miraculously emerge from the ground. Still, the sight of those improbable storefronts surely motivated me to look Upstairs and realize Hashem's Divine role in orchestrating the events, "successes," and yes, even the letdowns, of my career on this planet.

The *Chovos HaLevavos* adjures us to view our "days as scrolls" and to diligently hearken to the lessons they communicate. Along similar lines, my *rebbi*, Rav Moskovitz, counsels that the "*single* greatest lesson in *bitachon* is one's own life." Peruse the pages of your past and you'll find episode after episode of Hashem's involvement in the nitty-gritty details of life:

> The chapters of your life are the most compelling lessons in *bitachon*.

- Of checks you never expected to see (and yet you did)
- Of traffic you completely anticipated sitting in (and yet you didn't)
- Of flights you never thought you'd catch (and did)
- Of colds you totally expected to catch (and didn't)
- Of small problems (that became smaller) and large problems (that vanished altogether)
- Of stories one could never believe—and of stories that render it impossible *not* to believe

So get cracking on your own *megillah* today (if you wish you can call it the *Journal d'Eternal*). Keep your eyes open and let the chapters of your life (and your reflection thereon) serve as the catalyst to a keener perception of Hashem and the impetus to serve Him with a heightened dose of *emunah* and *simchah*.

Masei

Stop to Smell the Roses

While courting my bride-to-be, someone suggested that I should send flowers before Shabbos. Nice idea, I though...just one hitch. While "saying it with flowers" is often a terrific idea, this relationship was just *too* much of a delicate work-in-progress and my emotions just *too* scrambled for me to know exactly "what" I actually wanted my flowers to say.

Fortunately, Cliff (the customer service rep at 1-800-Flowers) was available to help me get a clear grip on my emotions so that I could effectively "say them with flowers." And so, on *erev Shabbos*, Cliff the customer service rep proceeded to educate me about the variety of bouquets and their associated meanings (of course, no one outside of 1-800-Flowers knows what each bouquet actually means, but I digress):

- How about carnations? Carnations say: "You're cute."
- How about violets? Violets mean: "I respect you."
- How about daffodils? Daffodils say: "I have a limited budget to spend on flowers."
- Poison ivy says: "You irritate me."
- Venus flytraps say, "You'd win most of our debates."

And so on and so forth. Anyway, I settled on irises, which supposedly say, "You're a really nice person and I have no clue where this is going but wanted to send you flowers anyway and hope the cholent is *gesh-mak.*" Perfect. Exactly what I wanted to get across. Cliff, where would I be without you?

As I was leaving for shul, the phone rang and my wife-to-be was on the other line, "Thank you *so* much for the flowers! They are beautiful and exquisite..." On and on. OK. Irises, check-plus. Nothing like "saying it with flowers." Cliff—you da man!

On Sunday morning, I picked my wife-to-be up at LaGuardia, only to find her toting several long-stem red roses. Great. Just my luck. I send a few measly irises and someone else trumps me with long-stem roses. "Aren't they beautiful?" she said. "There were twelve but I couldn't carry all of them on the plane. Oh well, I left the vase with my hosts, hope that was OK."

Uh-oh. A dozen long-stem red roses?! Vase?! It was apparent that my wife never received any irises (and the iris message); instead, she received a dozen long-stem roses (and the long-stem rose message!). I tried to play it cool but was clearly in over my head emotionally. As soon as I had the chance, I dialed 1-800-Flowers, demanding to speak with Cliff to discuss how much this blunder cost me. "Don't worry," he said. "Turns out we didn't have irises, so we afforded you a courtesy and bumped you up to a nicer bouquet. Same price!"

"Cliff," I hesitated, "that's great and I appreciate the thoughtful-ness...*but I think we're sending a different message here, aren't we?!*"

As anyone who has navigated the Level-6 white-water rapids of *shiddu-chim* and dating knows, the unpredictable is par for the course and the degree of *hashgachah pratis* (Divine Providence) is more readily discern-ible then life at large. So it was in our case, *baruch Hashem*, where my wife merited to receive long-stem roses, I merited to pay for irises, customer service rep Cliff managed to propel our courtship along, and, lo and be-hold, we found ourselves beneath the *chuppah* just a few months later.

These are the journeys of the Children of Israel...Moshe wrote their goings forth according to their journeys at the bidding of Hashem.

The odyssey of the wandering Jews and their forty-two encampments is part and parcel of the Torah and, as such, were *surely* written down by Moshe—just like the rest of the Torah. Did we think that Shakespeare inked these lines? Or perhaps some other travel writers (Marco Polo or Lewis and Clark)? Of course not. So why in the world did the Torah feel the need to remind us that Moshe was the scrivener here?

Faced with this question, the *Ohr HaChaim HaKadosh* explains that "Immediately after leaving Egypt, Hashem instructed Moshe to keep a running diary of their journeys as they occurred, and now, at the end of the forty-year odyssey, He told Moshe that his recordings were to become part of the Torah."

More than just a "Fodor's Guide to the Desert on Fifty *Shekalim* a Day," the Torah records the stops and starts and arrivals and departures, "to make known the acts of kindness of Hashem."[97] Rashi elaborates further with his well-known metaphor to "the journeys that a father traveled to nurture his son back to health," and his recollections thereof. Here you had a fever. Here you had a turn for the better…

As our lives unfold, we too find ourselves ricocheting from one situation to another. Certain eras of our lives are relatively tranquil, predictable, and conducive to growth, whereas others are chaotic, catch-as-catch-can and (also) conducive to growth—albeit of a different species. Periods of progress and periods of setbacks (and we can often grow even more from those setbacks). As we mull them over—be it contemporaneously or in retrospect—there is much, indeed, to be gleaned. For each of these ports of call offers their site-specific teachable moments for you to download on to your emotional hard drive; new perspectives on life and the human condition; and, ultimately, a greater clarity on what makes you tick (and makes you ticked off).

As Hashem shuttles us through life, remember to savor a few snapshots of *emunah* and *bitachon* and adorn them on your heart.

---

97   Rashi, *Bamidbar* 33:1.

The chapters of your life—the good, the bad, and the ugly, the highlights, the lowlights, and the seemingly no-lights, the best of times and the worst of times—ultimately comprise the very same chapters of the *sefer* that will teach you the greatest, most penetrating lessons in *emunah*. Each stage and phase amounts to your own personal *megillah*, replete with Hashem's handiwork at every turn.

So long as we are running the gauntlet of life, so long as the Travel Agency "Upstairs" is ushering us from vista to vista with the undying love of a parent concerned solely for our spiritual well-being, let us remember to take a few snapshots along the way and hang them—along with the profound messages they reveal—in the corridors of our mind. To revisit from time to time and thereby gain the ever-important (and ever-mercurial) *emunah* and *bitachon*, reliance and trust in Hashem—and the innate joy that is associated therewith.

Devarim

The Self-Help Section

S ome seventeen years ago, I commenced my short-lived stint as a litigator in a highly regarded, high-powered Manhattan law firm. The firm paid its associates a mint in exchange for (what felt like) every waking moment of our lives. The firm was like a metropolis unto itself—entirely dedicated to its clients (and the billable hours necessary to advocate vigorously on behalf of those clients). Just to get the flavor of the atmosphere: there was a graveyard shift of editors, so when I punched out at 9:45 p.m., I sent my documents upstairs to be proofread, and lo and behold, a red-marked copy was sitting on my desk upon my arrival the next morning.

Unfortunately, the salt-mine work hours produced a significant degree of stress (mitigated only somewhat by the Park Avenue paycheck). To combat this work-related anxiety, someone suggested that I purchase a book about "How to Breathe." (Sure enough, some Jewish fellow was making a fortune teaching the planet how to inhale and exhale). Apparently, if only I could breathe in through my left rib and out through my right ear, I could reconfigure my biorhythms and achieve perfect serenity and tranquility. For $17.99 it seemed like a good idea.

Eager to learn "How to Breathe," I inquired with Customer Service at Barnes & Noble where I could find this particular book, only to cringe upon hearing the response—"The Self-Help Section." Oh no...not there...anywhere but there...isn't that section for people who simply can't get a grip on life and are trying desperately to achieve some goal that has long eluded them (i.e., Troy McClure's classic *Smoke Your Way to Thinness* and *Get Confident, Stupid!*). In any event, I serpentined past that section, clandestinely hoping no one would recognize me, grabbed this treatise on breathing and proceeded to embark on a career of breathing that continues until this very day...

These are the words that Moshe spoke to all of Israel...

Rashi: "They are words of rebuke because the Torah lists all the places in which they caused anger before Hashem."[98]

The primary purpose of a man's life is to constantly strive to improve his character traits. Otherwise, what is life for?[99]

The focal point of *Sefer Devarim* is Moshe Rabbeinu's final discourse to his beloved nation—an address that commences with a veiled rebuke that references (albeit obliquely) the various low-water marks in our nation's fledgling career (the Golden Calf, Korach, the infamous reconnaissance mission to Eretz Yisrael, and so on and so forth). The purpose of Moshe's critique was to identify those areas in our national psyche—primarily *emunah* and *bitachon*—that needed refortification in order to meet the challenges that lay ahead.

In this respect, our willingness to identify, rectify, and rise above our imperfections is quite apropos for the Shabbos—Shabbos Chazon—that precedes the approaching Ninth of Av (and the particular *avodah* of that unique day on the Jewish calendar). Relatedly, the Alter from Kelm, Rav Simcha Zissel Ziv, explained the well-known Gemara (*Yoma* 9b) that contrasts the severe sins that preceded the destruction of the First Beis Hamikdash (murder, adultery, idol worship) with the

---

98   *Devarim* 1:1.
99   Vilna Gaon, *Even Sheleimah* (1:2).

seemingly less culpable sin of *sinas chinam* (baseless hatred and alienation among Jews) that brought about the destruction of the Second Beis Hamikdash, not to mention the ensuing 1900-plus years of exile.

The quintessential difference between those two eras, according to the Alter, is the degree to which Am Yisrael stood *omed l'hislamed*—ready to learn and improve. As such, the earlier generation's sincere desire to change eclipsed even the most severe misconduct. In contrast, the latter generation lacked that genuine impetus to change, and thus, even seemingly minor misdeeds loomed large. Their consequences rippled further into the future. Until this very day.

On Tishah b'Av we possess an opportunity (on both a national scope and on an individual level) to cultivate that sincere desire for self-help. While the very notion of self-help rings hollow and trite (at best) and downright dorky in most secular circles, it remains the coin of the realm for every Jew who is serious about turning themselves into a better person and, in turn, the world into a better world.

> Absent a genuine impetus to change, even relatively minor misdeeds can loom large.

These days can be long. These days can be unhurried. These days can be quiet. Indeed, they are days that present a rare opportunity for immense internal growth for those of us who stand *omed l'hislamed*.

Va'eschanan

Meet and Greet

Some seventy years ago or so, the Rosh Yeshiva of Etz Chaim, Rav Isser Zalman Meltzer, *zt"l*, heard his grandchildren hastily approaching his study. "Zeidy, Zeidy, the Chazon Ish is coming down the block. The Chazon Ish is coming! I think he is here to see you!" The Chazon Ish, of course, was none other than Rav Avraham Yeshaya Karelitz, the leading Torah sage of his time and venerable leader of Am Yisrael.

The rare opportunity to greet the *gadol ha'dor*, who was apparently visiting Yerushalayim from his home in B'nei Brak, sent the house into a tizzy. Rav Isser Zalman quickly donned his best Shabbos clothes, and the dining room table was adorned with a banquet-esque display of fruits, drinks, and decor. When a faint knock on the door was heard, the Meltzer family knew the awaited moment was imminent and prepared themselves to greet greatness.

Lo and behold, a gentleman *vaguely* resembling the Chazon Ish politely asked to speak with Rav Isser Zalman. Apparently, this forlorn individual was in dire financial straits and had no recourse other than to seek donations from others. To this end, he reckoned that a letter of recommendation or some quasi-formal endorsement from the pen of the illustrious Rav Isser Zalman would bolster his fund-raising efforts and lend some much-needed credibility with would-be donors.

Rav Isser Zalman graciously welcomed his visitor into the "grand" dining room. He regaled him with food and drink and patiently listened to his plight before inking a ringing endorsement of this gentleman's "cause" and sending him on his way amid blessings and well-wishes.

When the pauper left, one of the grandchildren hesitantly inquired, "Uh, Zeidy, you do know that wasn't the Chazon Ish right?!"

"Of course, my child...but doesn't *every* Jew deserve such a welcome?"

Ever experienced that awkward sensation when you've begun to convey your enthusiasm in seeing someone only to realize that, upon second thought, you don't actually have the foggiest notion who that person actually is? You thought it was an old acquaintance from your youth, but actually, it's just another fellow who looks a little bit similar. Oh well.

I've never seen the Etiquette Manual on how to navigate that one—do you confess, "Sorry, I thought you were someone else" or is it nobler to carry on the charade and pretend as if you're truly reunited with your long-lost buddy?

Forget about the façade of alienation that regrettably accompanies such superficial "identifications," such as what type of yarmulke a person wears, the length of his coat, the color of his shirt, or the pronunciation of his vowels and consonants. Truth be told, every one of us—without exaggeration—has so, so much in common with every single Jew they encounter. Take the Chabadnik you pass in the airport. Take the Bukharian barber. Take the Israeli cab driver. Or that guy who's going to ask you for *tzedakah* on Sunday morning. Don't you share the same past? Don't you share the same mission on earth (i.e., to be a light unto the nations)? Don't your Friday afternoons resemble one another in their hustle and bustle? Don't your Friday nights resemble one another in their calmness and sanctity?

> Peer beyond the façade of alienation and discover how much you have in common with your fellow Jew.

Let's make this period after Tishah b'Av a time for camaraderie and a broader sense of identity—one with enough emotional bandwidth to love Jews of all stripes and to communicate that message of togetherness.

Heels and Souls

As part and parcel of their Sunday afternoon festivities, eighty thousand-plus fans packed into Giants Stadium simultaneously went bananas as the mega screen offered instant replay after instant replay of the play that had just transpired. Seems the Giants' lumbering tight end caught a pass and managed, somehow, to grind out another three yards (enough for an elusive and improbable first down), notwithstanding three voracious defenders who were singularly focused on wrestling him to the ground.

Every angle you can imagine captured these heroic footsteps—from the sideline, from the end zone, from the blimp. Again and again, each replay was accompanied with a roar that could be heard throughout northern New Jersey.

Now, what's the big deal, really?! We all walk three yards all the time and no one's offering us any standing ovations. I walk from the kitchen to the den effortlessly and there is no applause. I walk to shul and no one's impressed. Even a sedentary person takes three thousand steps (at least) each day.

The answer, obviously, is that some steps loom larger than others.

A baby's first steps are commemorated with pictures and applause and emails to proud grandparents the world over.

In July 1969, 238,000 miles away, Neil Armstrong took "one small step for man, one giant leap for mankind."

And it will be because [eikev] of your listening to these ordinances, and your observing and performing them that Hashem, your G-d, will...love you, He will bless you and He will multiply you...[100]

Rashi explains that *eikev* (a word that lends itself to various meanings) refers to the "relatively light commandments that a person tramples with their *heels*" (*eikev* in Hebrew).

From the Torah's perspective, everyday footsteps can amount to greatness. We need not schlep defenders downfield in front of the masses. We need not spearhead any lunar missions to achieve greatness. The benchmark of a Yid is his or her capacity to achieve *shleimus*, completion, and such is the by-product of consistently striving to live virtuously. To live with gratitude. To perceive goodness in the world (and in others). To seek out kindliness. To live with integrity. A smile here. A kind word there. No one has to know. Are they important? Absolutely. Are they headline-grabbers? Usually not.

The Torah's road to shleimus is traversed with everyday footsteps.

Indeed, the coin of the Torah realm lies in our *everyday* lives. In our daily footsteps. Each one represents a tremendous blessing. Each one presents a tremendous opportunity. For within our everyday footsteps lies the path to true greatness. When we cultivate an appreciation for each step, we will find those very steps can propel us to wondrous "feats."

---

100 *Devarim* 7:12–13.

Re'eh

Summer
Spirits

Scene 1

With a mix of anticipation and trepidation, the parents tear open their son's first letter from sleepaway camp:

1 July, 2017

Dear Mom and Dad,

I wish I could say camp is fun. It's not. I always get picked last for the basketball games. It's colder than you said it would be and I'm a popsicle at night. Also, the canteen doesn't have blue sour sticks.

Can I come home?

Your unhappy son

Gulp. Hit the *Tehillim*. Where's that number for the 24-hour *tzedakah* hotline? Hold out for some glimmer of hope. Pounce on the mailman the next day to see if things have improved...

2 July, 2017

Dear Mom and Dad,

Don't have time to write. Camp is the best. Coach Kleinberg

149

worked with me on my jump shot and I wasn't picked last. He let me take the last shot, and guess what? I made it!! Chaim from Toronto claims he's cold-blooded. Anyway, he lent me his blanket at night so it's nice to be warm. Also, Yitzchak is now in charge of the canteen and there are lots of blue sour sticks. Can I stay for second session?

Your elated son

Hooray. *Baruch Hashem*! Hit the *Tehillim* again. Double that *tzedakah* pledge. Who is this Coach Kleinberg and does he have a Chase QuickPay account?! I'd like to wire him an "early" tip. Thank G-d for Chaim from Toronto—Hashem should bless him with all that's good in this world and the next. And get a letter out pronto to the Camp Director recommending that Yitzchak at the canteen receive a promotion and a raise. Maybe I know a good *shidduch* for him...

Scene 2

To pass the time on a lazy August Sunday, Mommy suggests that her kids operate a lemonade stand in their residential cul-de-sac. Financially speaking, it's a short-sighted idea and a by-product of Mommy's lack of economic forecasting. After all, the suburban side road barely gets *any* traffic besides the local residents. But it's a nice, inexpensive, and wholesome activity. Hours roll by. No one has even stopped. The ice has melted. The kids-turned-entrepreneurs are wilting. Frustration-driven tantrums are somewhat expected at this point.

Given the dearth of customers and the dwindling profit margin, Mom is busy preparing her consolation speech to buoy her kids' broken spirits. "Our job is just to try. The rest is up to Hashem. You did your best and that's all one can do. Tomorrow, maybe we'll practice filing for Chapter 11!" Wait. Hold the phone. Mommy hears the voices of elated children holding a stack of dollar bills. Seems a circa-1992 maroon Dodge Caravan stopped off and bought up the entire stock of lemonade.

Mommy wonders, "Who was that driver? Anyone get a look at the license plate? Thank you. Thank you. You made my kids day! G-d bless you and watch over you and keep you. Your Caravan should last *another* hundred thousand miles and fit plenty of car seats. All *your* investments should be profitable…"

You shall surely give him [your fellow Jew in need], and let your heart not feel bad when you give him, for because of this matter, Hashem, your G-d, will bless you in all your deeds and in your every undertaking.[101]

You shall rejoice before Hashem, your God—you, your [household], the Levite who is in your cities, the convert, the orphan, and the widow who are among you.
Rashi: "If you will make Mine happy (i.e., the Levite, convert, orphan, and widow) I will make yours [i.e., your household] happy."[102]

When someone—even a total stranger—bestows a kindness upon a loved one, we innately feel a deep-seated kinship and sincere debt of gratitude for his or her sensibilities that were ultimately responsible for easing the plight of someone very near and dear. Be it Coach Kleinberg's willingness to work on a sub-par jump shot and thereby instill much-needed confidence. Be it a thoughtful camper's willingness to share his blanket. Be it the canteen supplier who lifted the spirits of a forlorn camper. Be it some unknown patron who (with a few minutes and a few dollars) injected a much-needed dosage of *simchah*, enthusiasm, and positivity into Team Lemonade. These not-uncommon summer vignettes offer a glimpse into what our *chessed* means—not just to the recipient—but in the eyes of Hashem, our Father Upstairs.

---

101   *Devarim* 15:10.
102   Ibid. 16:11.

Imagine a guest of yours walking home from a Shabbos meal. Satiated, he or she looks heavenward and says, "Hashem, I just wanted to tell you that I had no idea where I'd be eating this Shabbos and a wonderful family invited me into their home and served a delicious cholent and even gave me a second piece of cake." Far be it from us to know the ways of Hashem, but it is entirely logical and plausible for us to at least estimate the love and appreciation and goodwill Hashem would direct toward those very hosts who took in his lonely "child" for this Shabbos meal.

Ditto for when we dance at someone's wedding; we are doing more than living up to social etiquette; rather, we are causing one of Hashem's children to rejoice. When we help another Jew who is having a rough go of things financially, we are helping instill confidence and optimism into one of Hashem's children. Can we estimate what a *nachas* that must be in the eyes of Hashem?

Chessed is more than helping another Jew, it's about caring for Hashem's beloved child.

For those on the lookout, opportunities abound for us to answer the call. *Chessed* is more than just helping another Jew—it's buoying the spirits of Hashem's beloved child.

Shoftim

Fighting
Words

I n 1976, America was introduced to a new hero, Rocky Balboa—the "underdog" personified—who achieved unimagined accomplishments in the boxing ring. One of the linchpins of Rocky's success was the grit, gruff, and dogged determination of his trainer, Mickey Goldmill (of Jewish descent, of course), who was admired for his old-fashioned training techniques and uncanny knack of conveying profound thoughts from amid the blood, sweat, tears, and rough-and-tumble of the boxing ring. Perhaps Mickey's most memorable words came after an exhausted and near-lifeless Rocky had been knocked out and yet was inspired to muster every last ounce of strength to get up from the canvas...Why? Because he heard Mickey's heartfelt pleas to "Get up, Rocky! Get up!...Because Mickey loves ya!"

While few (if any) of us have endured a heavyweight boxing match, life can sometimes feel like we're fending off jabs and dodging knockout punches round after round. For one seeking to survive such ordeals, the sincere and inspirational words of a trusted confidant can be invaluable in the quest to unearth latent inner strength and unlock untapped potential.

Even when navigating life's "tamer" seas, the short- and long-term emotional and psychological benefits of sincere *divrei chizuk* are inestimable.

For instance, in a very different context, a young lady (twelve or so) was seeking clarity on certain Torah perspectives (some macro, lofty concepts and other micro, nitty-gritty details). In the hopes of addressing these particular questions, the parents coordinated a meeting between their daughter and a highly regarded Rav, known far and wide for the breadth and depth of his insight and wisdom. After giving generously of his time and thoroughly addressing each of her inquiries in an age-appropriate fashion, the Rav proceeded to thank her for coming and concluded by saying, "I am very proud to have such a young woman with such sensibilities in my shul." Those choice words from such an *adam gadol* under such circumstances could very well have provided a wellspring of self-confidence for years to come. Were they essential? No. Were they inspiring? Absolutely. Did they generate self-assuredness? Undoubtedly.

Against this backdrop, we can readily appreciate the role that the Torah assigns to certain field generals that accompany Am Yisrael into battle. They are not infantrymen. Nor are they archers or medics. Rather, Rashi describes these personnel as "uprighters" who "stand at the edge of the battle formation to raise upright those who are fallen and to strengthen them verbally, saying, "Go back to the battle and do not flee!"[103] The Torah finds these individuals worthy of mention and identifies them as a crucial component of the war effort.

I venture to say that each of us could effortlessly identify a half dozen people who are grappling with challenges (emotional, financial,

---

103 *Devarim* 20:9.

physical, familial, etc.), who could be inspired to "get back in the ring" if they were privy to hear the right words from the right person at the right time. Can you play the role of the "uprighter" in their life? Can you strike the right chord that will inspire another to "get up" and get back in the ring?

Don't underestimate your capacity to unearth hidden capacities in others. Your words may just be the key to their success and the emotional octane necessary to propel them forward in their personal struggle to persevere.

Don't underestimate the impact your words can have on those seeking to persevere against the tide of personal struggles.

Ki Seitzei

Beyond a Shadow of a Doubt

O n September 25, 1983, I spent my ninth birthday doing what I loved best—watching the New York Jets. Not just from the comforts of home, but rather from the bleachers at Shea Stadium alongside fifty-two thousand fellow fans decked out in the green and white of their beloved squad. The Los Angeles Rams were in town and, a true birthday gift, the game was headed into overtime.

As the placekicker lined up for what would prove to be the winning field goal, a beer-induced, haunting bellow emerged from behind us. "YOU CAN'T DO-OO IT! YOU CAN'T DO-OO IT!" Indeed, one courageous (and/or inebriated and ill-advised) Rams' supporter was seeking to get "into the kicker's jug" (as the expression goes), rattle his nerves, and somehow try to shake his confidence. Of course, when the ball split the uprights, ensuring a Jets' victory, this fellow's sinister plans and amateur attempt at psychological warfare came to an abrupt halt. Apparently, the kicker *could* do it. And did.

On the other side of the spectrum, we find Watty Piper (aka Arnold Munk) who, in 1930, introduced the world to that never-say-die *Little Engine That Could*. For those of you who failed "Great American Children's Stories," the storyline is as follows. When a train carrying "all good things" stalls unexpectedly at the base of a mountain, the hopes of a timely delivery to "the good little boys and girls on the other side of the mountain" are seemingly squashed. (Apparently, this was before the days of Amazon Prime). When the "Shiny New Engine," "Passenger Engine," and "Big Strong Engine" find excuses why they can't finish the task, the situation looks bleak from the viewpoint of even the rosiest-colored-glasses.

Alas, along comes "Little Blue Engine," who is short on talent (after all, he has "never been over the mountain") but long on courage. Inspired by the "thought of the good little boys and girls on the other side of the mountain, who would have no toys and no wholesome foods unless she helped," Little Blue Engine sets out to climb that mountain with the precious cargo in tow. Lacking experience. Low on strength. Skeptical observers yelling "You can't do-oo it!" (Actually, that detail might just be my ad-libbing.) In any event, facing no shortage of reasons to throw in the towel (as her predecessors had), Little Blue Engine proceeds to climb that peak fueled by one drive and one motto: "I think I can—I think I can—I think I can." And indeed, when her unlikely objective has been achieved, the book concludes with a tribute to that never-say-die attitude, "I thought I could. I thought I could."

Of course, Little Blue Engine makes it, the "little boys and girls on the other side of the mountain" get their goodies. The "big mommies and daddies on the other side of the mountain" are (probably) greatly relieved that they don't have to run out to Toys R' Us at the eleventh hour (or sue the train company for breach of contract) and Americans have yet another folk legend with which to inspire generations of youngsters (me included) about how much is possible (or perhaps, more accurately, how few things are *impossible*) so long as you "think you can."

> *Remember what Amalek did to you, on the way when you were leaving Egypt.*[104]

Amalek, the archenemy of Am Yisrael, represents the antithesis of all that we stand for and aspire to accomplish in this world. At the forefront of Amalek's sinister schemes to halt our personal (and national) progress and determination is the innate and incessant capacity to sow the seeds of doubt in our hearts and minds.

Our capacity to strive for (and undertake) greater levels of commitment and dedication—be it in the realm of our own observance, our core relationships, our professional ambitions, our pursuit of wisdom, our understanding of *emes*, or our general willingness to improve—constitutes our personal voyage out of our personal Egypt. And that is precisely where Amalek seeks to interfere. To be sure, the path to perfection in each of these realms is laden with Amalek's arsenal of "doubtfulness" and that haunting inner voice that reminds us "You can't do-oo it!"

Silence the inner voice of self-doubt with the realization that Hashem is rooting for your success.

When we strengthen our resolve in *Avinu She'baShamayim*, namely, that Hashem is indeed *schepping* major *nachas* from us as we climb the mountain of personal (and national) growth—and furthermore, is *rooting* for us to achieve and succeed—we can eradicate those doubts amid a resounding, sincere, robust reminder that "I think I can!" (And Hashem surely can!)

As we systematically eliminate those waves of self-doubt, we will invariably experience an immensely satisfying degree of *simchah* (as the saying goes, "There is no *simchah* like the resolution of doubt."). This *simchah* can, in turn, fuel our *avodah* as well as the motivation to inspire others to keep on trucking.

---

104 *Devarim* 25:17.

Ki Savo

Service
with a Smile

I n the aftermath of September 11, America—a country that boasts vast and extensive outlets for leisure and recreation—donned a sobering attitude toward its national pastimes. Commissioner Selig suspended Major League Baseball for the first time since D-day. The Emmy Awards slated for September 16 were postponed until October 7 (and did not air until November). En masse corporate outings, sporting events, and concerts were canceled, and sea to shining sea—New York especially—there was a palpable shift in the nation's psyche.

Just several weeks later, I celebrated Sukkos in Boston, where Rav Moskovitz queried (rhetorically) whether or not Am Yisrael should, in keeping with that tenor, cancel Sukkos, our *zman simchaseinu* (the time of our happiness). Obviously, Sukkos went on as scheduled, just as it had for time immemorial, irrespective of whether the "times" were more robust or more bleak. The best of times or the worst of times.

The rationale, the Rav explained, can be found in the *Chumash* and the Divine architecture that unites seemingly disparate themes. Specifically, the Torah enumerates a lengthy and frightening description of what may befall Am Yisrael should they sever their connection with Hashem and fail to discharge their unique mission in this world. Smack in the middle there, one verse pinpoints *the* precise catalyst for this parade of horrible as follows, "Because you did not serve Hashem, your G-d, amid gladness and goodness of heart, when everything was abundant."[105] The verses then abruptly revert back to the admonition until their conclusion.

Had you or I been narrating these verses, the Rav explained, it stands to reason that the "reason" for the curse should have appeared either up front (i.e., "and if you don't serve Hashem amid gladness...this shall befall you") or at the end (i.e., "and all this shall befall you...if you don't serve Hashem amid gladness"). So what exactly is the Torah conveying to us by inserting the deciding factor in the *middle*?

The answer, the Rav proclaimed, lies in the unswerving capacity for a Jew to serve Hashem with joy *regardless* of circumstances. Even when the world seems to be crumbling under your feet and the walls are caving in (literally, symbolically, emotionally, financially, etc.), one should know that the innate and inseverable connection we maintain with Hashem remains viable and vibrant. It remains capable of propelling us not just to *avodas Hashem*, but to true and sincere *simchah* in that very *avodas Hashem*.

With the proper perspective, a Jew can always serve Hashem with *simchah* — regardless of the circumstances.

As the *Chovos HaLevavos*, *Ramban*, and others explain, the foundation of the Torah rests on the pillars of gratitude—to vividly recall the myriad blessings we were all privy to: life itself and all that's in it. Taking these abundant kindnesses into account, one can acquire—with relative ease—a heightened appreciation for Hashem's endless desire to bestow goodness upon His beloved creatures. This awareness alone surely constitutes a priceless acquisition for the new year.

---

105   *Devarim* 28:47.

Nitzavim

Dedication
Opportunities
Available

One summer, I had an unexpected opportunity to chat with one of the directors of a camp for children with special needs—a bastion of *chessed* and selflessness, dedicated to bringing smiles and good times to children with special needs and their families.

"So, how many campers attend?" I inquired en route to shul.

"All told, about three hundred."

"Wow. And how many do you have on staff?"

"About five hundred."

"Unbelievable. What an operation! What a responsibility! And, let me ask you a question: In your estimation, what's the difference between a *good* counselor and a *great* counselor?"

"Simple," he responded, "You can tell in fifteen seconds. A good counselor will do what you ask of them. And I have no problem with that whatsoever. A great counselor, though, is totally and completely dedicated to the needs and well-being of the camper or campers he is responsible for."

Having been sick for several days, our two-year-old's cries indicated she was in increasingly more pain. Nothing in our medicine cabinet would effectively numb the sores in her mouth. Just several hours before Shabbos, my wife rang the pediatrician one last time to see if the staff had any other recommendations how to soothe our little Sara Sosha. Our pediatrician, Dr. Gewirtz, himself *shomer Shabbos*, proceeded to call in one last prescription to a local pharmacy. I waited and waited, but alas, the pharmacist informed me that they did not carry that medication, nor would it be available until the next day. So much for that idea.

Dr. Gewirtz didn't stop there, however. Despite the fact that his office was now closed and *his* Shabbos was rapidly approaching, he called (this time from his home) to a second pharmacy. It seemed they would be able to turn it around for us before candle-lighting time. I jetted down to pharmacy number two. When I arrived, Dr. Gewirtz's new prescription was already being attended to, however...there was a glitch in the store's computer system and the codes for the medication weren't registering properly.

Rather than saying, "Hey, I tried. I called two pharmacies...it's twenty-five minutes to Shabbos...Good luck and call me on Sunday!" our pediatrician stayed on the line again and again and again to try to get the medication's "coordinates" to synchronize with CVS's internal codes. Finally...voilà...the codes matched up, the prescription could be filled (finally), and the good doctor could have an uninterrupted nanosecond to get ready for Shabbos. (And no, there was no extra charge for this after-hours, moments-before-Shabbos dedication to his patient.)

You are standing here today...to pass into a covenant of Hashem...and into His oath that Hashem...forges with you today, in order to establish you today as a people to Him and that He be a G-d to you.[106]

---

106 *Devarim* 29:9–12.

In his final hours of life, Moshe Rabbeinu diligently attended to the last task on his agenda (and perhaps the most important)—the singular task of forging an eternal covenant between Hashem and Am Yisrael.

A pact that would transcend time and endure forever.

A *bris* that would transcend space and survive wherever.

A bond that would unite all Jews and their Maker.

An unbreakable pact premised on each and every Jew's commitment to render his or her own personal agenda a distant second to Hashem's national (and world) agenda.

We are *all* members of that covenant. We all carry the responsibilities (and rewards) of living up to that covenant and perpetuating its ideals. The Torah does not look kindly upon the one who assuages "himself in his heart saying, 'I will have peace, though I go as my heart sees fit,'" which Rashi explains as, "I do what my heart sees fit to do."[107]

Strength, as we know, can be measured in myriad ways. The strength of a person is gauged by how many pounds he can hoist. The strength of a sound, by the distance from which it can heard. The strength of a relationship, however, is measured at the end of the day by the degree of *dedication* that the parties harbor toward one another. In a word—it comes down to commitment.

One noted printing company is quick to remind its clients, "At Dick Bailey, we are *fully committed* to your success." When I read that I wonder, can I say that about myself—that I am fully committed to anyone else's success? I don't even know if I'm fully committed to *my* success!

Ask yourself: Am I *fully committed* to my relationship with Hashem? With the bond that Moshe forged for me? With Hashem's vision of success for mankind?

May we all merit to rededicate ourselves to that *bris* and to the extent we can renew our total commitment to that covenant, so may we enjoy and merit lives full of health, peace, and *berachah*.

---

107   Ibid. 29:18.

Vayeilech

Teaching
Teaching

Awhile ago, I presented a lecture that I (in my totally un-
biased, completely objective, not-so-humble opinion) felt
was insightful, informative, interesting, and inspiring.
That being said, the blank faces on the attendees that night
suggested that perhaps my presentation would be better described as
lackluster, scatterbrained, disjointed, and in need of revamping. What
happened over here?

To my great fortune, a senior *mechanech* who has been teaching Torah
to hundreds of students over dozens of years was privy to the class. The
next day, I followed up with him to seek some meaningful feedback and
constructive criticism. "Well," he asked, "what point(s) were you trying
to convey in the class?" (Lesson Number 1: Always identify in your own
mind *the* core message you are seeking to get across. And if *you* don't
have clarity on what that core message is, then you can bet that your
listeners surely don't know what you're really driving at.)

I mentioned a couple of the main ideas that I was hoping to communicate and wondered why they seemingly got lost in translation.
"Always remember," he told me, "just because you *gave* a class doesn't
necessarily mean that anyone *heard* a class."

We all strive to be erudite and polished. Witty and entertaining.
Astute and insightful. But what truly matters, when push comes to

shove, is *not* how many highfalutin words you uttered, but rather whether or not your message actually hit home. For if you're cruising at a higher (or different) intellectual altitude than those in your orbit, your effectiveness as an educator will undoubtedly suffer.

Gather together the people—the men and the women and the small children, and your stranger who is in your cities—so that they will hear and so that they will learn, and they shall fear Hashem, your G-d, and be careful to perform all the words of this Torah. And their children who do not know—they shall hear and they shall learn to fear Hashem, your G-d, all the days that you live on the land to which you are crossing the Jordan, to take possession of it.[108]

So now, write this song for yourselves, and teach it to the Children of Israel, place it in their mouth.[109]

I will make my way at my slow pace according to...the gait of the children.[110]

Rashi: By the pace at which they are able to walk.

It is imperative to view ourselves as teachers. (And yes, we are all teachers—regardless of whether we possess tenure, have a roll book, or hold parent-teacher conferences.) Some teach children and grandchildren. Others impart knowledge to nieces, nephews, and cousins. We may have formal (or less-formal) "students" (of all ages) to whom we yearn to enrich with wisdom and understanding. We educate

> It is imperative to view ourselves as teachers. (And yes, we are all teachers.)

---

108 *Devarim* 31:12–13.
109 Ibid. 31:19.
110 *Bereishis* 33:14.

clients and colleagues and friends and acquaintances.

That being said, it behooves us to reassess (at least periodically) the degree to which we are capitalizing upon our "teaching" opportunities. Educating others has always been fraught with challenges—and it doesn't seem to be getting any easier. The process is quite astonishing, really. How is it that a concept (stored away somewhere in our vast cerebral cortex) can properly be understood and articulated in a way that it will lodge properly in the mind and heart of the person with whom we are communicating? The likelihood of being misunderstood is so vast. The risk of being unclear lurks behind virtually every byte of information you seek to present. What is clear and unequivocal to you is often cluttered and objectionable by the time it reaches someone *else*'s think pad.

As a trial attorney once coached, if you hope to win your case, you have to try and reach *everyone* in that jury box individually. You have to reach them *where they are*. One guy possesses the intellectual prowess of Homer Simpson. One woman thinks in terms of lofty ideals of social justice. To the degree you can assess how someone *else* processes the world, that is a very reliable gauge of the extent to which your message will hit the mark.

When the panel of judges are peppering you with inquiries, those truly skilled in the art of appellate advocacy are invariably cool under fire. Why? Because they (1) know their case inside and out and (2) are endeavoring to answer *more* than just a question—but to answer the questioner. What's ticking in this judge's mind that makes this particular matter troublesome? What's *behind* this specific question?

How the lesson is conveyed is as important (if not more) than what lesson is conveyed.

As "teachable moments" present themselves—and surely they will—be mindful of the awesome opportunity and responsibility that lies before you. Even when you know your information. Even when you know the lesson. *How* it is conveyed, however, will make all the difference. One person needs a parable. Another needs a story. One person thinks in the abstract stratospheres of spirituality while another functions only in terms of the practical "bottom line."

The Torah's recipe for effective *chinuch* is built on the notion (indeed the challenge and responsibility) that teachers must find a way to bring truth to wherever their students may be. Just because you gave over a message doesn't mean that it was *heard*. And just because it was heard doesn't mean that it truly hit home. Give it some thought—for all those who stand to learn from your ways have so much to gain.

Haazinu

Special Delivery

Sometimes you want to go…

Where everybody knows your name

and they're always glad you came…

Had I not known otherwise, I would have thought Gary Portnoy's now-famous lyrics were discussing a quaint, beloved shul in Huntington, New York. What the shul lacks in population density, it more than makes up for with warmth, selflessness, and *mesirus nefesh*. Led by a rav and rebbetzin of uncommon *ahavas Yisrael* that filters down to the shul's members, you're likely to feel *right* at home, *right* away. If you have the privilege to visit, I'm sure you'll also attest that "everybody will know your name, and they're always glad you came…"

From a historian's standpoint, ask anyone "in the know" how this congregation (now in its third decade) came to be and they'll tell you, "It's an amazing story." And believe it or not, it all started with a…swastika, of all things. As our Sages say, "*Harbeh shluchim l'Makom*—Hashem has no shortage of messengers."

Yes, some thirty years ago, the lone Torah Day School in Suffolk County was vandalized and several swastikas were graffitied onto the premises' walls. A painful reminder that (even with the First Amendment's guarantees of "Freedom of Religion") the American Jew (or Jew in America, as the case may be) is still in exile.

Who the perpetrator was we'll never know. Perhaps it was some disgruntled youth not fully cognizant of how that dreaded symbol tears at a Jews' heartstrings. Perhaps it was a deranged neo-Nazi interested in perpetuating the hate of yesteryear. Whoever it was and whatever the motivation, *no one* in their wildest dreams could have imagined the ripple effects this seemingly isolated act of indifference would have on generations of Yidden.

For these swastikas ultimately brought dozens and dozens of Jewish families back to Torah observance. That bloodcurdling symbol of cruelty set into motion a Divinely inspired chain of events that forged deep, meaningful relationships between the school's principal (and his rebbetzin) and several Huntington families open (and eager) to learn more about the Torah and its timeless wisdom—the knowledge of which they simply were not privy to while growing up. Deeply impressed with the heretofore undiscovered *chochmah* and *emes* of Torah and the beauty and meaningfulness of a Torah life, these few families embarked on a most improbably journey toward observance.

Without doing justice (whatsoever) to the remarkable developments that ultimately launched the shul, suffice to say that the shul's continued existence is a remarkable *kiddush Hashem*. In hindsight (and the legend is *still* unfolding), we see how those very swastikas were the unlikely catalyst for thousands of *tefillos* that have gone up to *Shamayim*. We see how those very swastikas spawned the sweet sound of Torah study that has reverberated through Suffolk County, Long Island, inspiring *neshamos* of all ages and stages and walks of life. We see how those swastikas—the very symbol most closely associated with the *absence* of Godliness in our midst—has sowed the seeds of a community whose very existence is an inspiring testament to the *sanctification* of Godliness in our midst.

G-d will then take up the cause of His people and comfort His servants. He will have seen that their power is gone, with nothing left to keep or abandon.[111]

Rashi: "When He will see that the hand of the enemy becomes progressively much stronger against them."

Hashem sent from on high and took me, He drew me out of deep waters. He saved me from my mighty foe and from my enemies that overpowered me. They confronted me on the day of my misfortune, but Hashem was my support.[112]

I recall Rav Nachman Bulman, *zt"l*, teaching us *Shir HaShirim* and the inimitable emotional surge that came over him upon reaching the verse stating: "I bind you [nations of the world] under oath...that you do not cause hatred, nor disturb this love [between Me and My beloved Am Yisrael] while I still find her pleasing.[113]

Rav Bulman thundered, "Nations! You'll see, if you start up with My beloved People while I still love them...you'll see...you'll drive them right back to Me!"

"If you start up with My beloved People while I still love them...you'll drive them right back to Me!"

For those of us privy to the *teshuvah* movement of recent decades, we are literally astounded by the droves and droves of heretofore unaffiliated Jews—college students, young professionals, middle-agers, and seniors—who have heeded the call to reclaim their Jewish roots. This miraculous en masse return to observance—unprecedented in Jewish history—is unfolding on the streets of LA, Buenos Aires, and Cape Town. On Californian campuses and the corridors of European universities. In a nutshell...a Divinely inspired return from out of a vast, barren spiritual wasteland.

Be it a geographic exile, a political one, or one's own personal sense

---

111   *Devarim* 32:36.
112   *Shmuel* II, 17–19, *Haftarah* to *Haazinu*.
113   *Shir HaShirim* 2:7.

of estrangement or lack of belonging, the Torah repeatedly reminds us that to a Jew, no matter how deep the exile (seems to be), no matter how aimless the wandering (appears to be), it is merely the raw material from which to forge an empowering, enriching, and vibrant relationship with Hashem and Am Yisrael, whom He will never forsake.

This notion lies at the heart of the Torah's *nechamah*. To know that exile is always purposeful and that true connectedness to our Maker is always available for those who seek it. This knowledge that Hashem is waiting for each of us, from amid our own exile, can provide ample foundation upon which to rededicate our relationship with Hashem.

> Exile is always purposeful, and true connectedness to our Maker is always available to those who seek it.

V'zos Haberachah

Brotherly Love

In 1965, the family-owned Monsey Kosher Bake Shop opened its doors on 51 Main Street in the then sparsely populated hamlet of Monsey. For decades thereafter, they serviced the Monsey community and Rockland County at large, supplying one and all with delectable challahs, yummy rugelach, and pastries of all types. Known far and wide as "Mrs. Frank's Bakery," the proprietors faithfully supplied a great "knead" and presumably made quite a bit of "dough" along the way. (OK, enough puns for now.)

One day, a new bakery announced its grand opening, of all places, on 40 Main Street, virtually across the street from Frank's. I did not call Monsey home at the time, nor did I ever discuss the matter with the proprietor's from Frank's, but one can only imagine the superhuman strength necessary *not* to harbor ill will toward the "new kid on the block," which—in the eyes of even an amateur economist—would inevitably siphon off customers (and profits). How many rereads of the *Gate of Trust* would suffice to silence basic principles of capitalism—i.e., that Frank's cash register would be *more* stuffed *but for* the bakery across the street?

One Thursday evening, many years later, a fire broke out in the small shopping strip at 40 Main Street. The damage was extensive and several stores had no choice but to relocate. And yet, the very next morning, *erev Shabbos*, the busiest day of the week by far, the 40 Main Street Bakery was somehow able to service its customers via a makeshift, street-side, temporary "storefront," replete with challahs, rugelach, and cookies. How was this feasible given last night's blaze and the destruction it caused to their ovens and production area?

You guessed it. When the owners of Frank's Bakery learned of the fire, they empathized with the plight of their "competitor," and in an act of remarkable selflessness, graciously invited the 40 Main Street bakery personnel to utilize Frank's *own* ovens (after hours) in order to service their loyal 40 Main Street customers the next morning. No grudge. No "what goes around comes around." No "all's fair in war and business." Just a sincere, deep-seated sense of connection with one's fellow Yidden and an unadulterated desire to alleviate their plight.

> *And He became King over Yeshurun when the numbers of the nation are gathered—the tribes of Israel in unity.*
>
> Rashi: *"When they are gathered together in a single group and there is peace among them, He is their King, but not when there is discord among them."*[114]

To a significant degree, the opening chapters of our nation's history are preoccupied with relationships (or the lack thereof) among siblings. Yitzchak and Yishmael. Yaakov and Eisav. Leah and Rachel. Yosef and his brothers. Beyond that, those who process history through spiritual lenses view large segments of our nation's exile as an outgrowth and repercussion of the Yaakov-Eisav paradigm.

The bitterness of this sibling rivalry was mitigated, somewhat, just two generations later, with the fraternal relationship between Yosef's sons, Ephraim and Menasheh. Indeed, many a Shabbos meal the world over commences with a blessing upon one's son(s) with the heartfelt aspiration that "Hashem make you like Ephraim and Menasheh." Of all

---

114 *Devarim* 33:5.

the role models in our nation's history, why do these two represent the gold standard of *Yiddishe nachas*?

Rav Noach Weinberg, *zt"l*, explains,

> *The relationship of Ephraim and Menasheh epitomizes the way brothers should love and trust each other. When Yaakov gave the younger brother, Ephraim, the favored blessing, Menasheh, the firstborn, could have protested and resented his brother for taking what was rightfully his, but Menasheh said nothing. He understood that what matters most is not his position or status, but rather what is best for the Jewish People. We bless our sons to emulate Ephraim and Menasheh because their relationship was without any trace of resentment. They are our role models.*[115]

Our perception of the Jewish People is often (regrettably) one of divisiveness and disunity. Be it Israeli politics or various sects of Torah-observant Jews adhering to their own unique *minhagim*, a deep-seated sense of oneness often eludes us. At times like this, it behooves us to conjure up a snapshot of Jewish brotherhood at its best—be it Ephraim and Menasheh, David and Yonasan, or Frank's Bakery.

At the end of the day, what is *the* explanation for the centuries-long exile? Our Sages tell us it is on account of *sinas chinam*, an estrangement, alienation, and hatred of one Jew for his spiritual "brother."[116] Amid great fanfare, celebration, and camaraderie, the conclusion of the *Chumash* provides a unique opportunity to reassess our own personal connectedness and dedication (or lack thereof) to our fellow Jews' well-being. What do our relationships *really* look like, and what they *could* (and *should*) look like if we could just diffuse the jealousy, one-upmanship,

> At our core, we all share a common bond—to advance the mission of our Torah, *chessed*, and *emes* that our ancestors strived to achieve.

---

115 *Wisdom for Living* (Shaar Press, 2015), pp. 77–78.
116 *Yoma* 9b.

and petty emotional baggage that threatens to put so much static on the line.

We are reminded that, at our core, we are all brothers and sisters who share in the perpetuation of the Torah, *chessed*, and *emes*—the very same mission as that of our ancestors. As we finish our annual odyssey through the *Chumash*, may we capitalize on the opportunity to renew our dedication to one another and imbue ourselves with a renewed commitment to *shalom* and *ahavas Yisrael*.

Mo'adim

Pesach

The Nitty-Gritty Details

One can often gauge the significance of an event by the extent to which the nitty-gritty details can be recalled and the vividness of that recollection. For instance, people can instantly recall where they were when they heard the incredulous news that the World Trade Center was under terrorist attack. Mothers know the weight of their children at birth. People can describe the weather on their wedding day and the details of how and when they first met their spouse.

The more one tells about the Exodus, the more he is praiseworthy.[117]

A common theme that weaves its way through the Haggadah is our attention to detail. A "story" that could be conveyed in two minutes—"We were slaves to Pharaoh in Mitzrayim. Hashem brought us

---

117 Haggadah.

out in a miraculous fashion to make us His nation forever and ever, and blessed us with the privilege of keeping His Torah and serving as a light unto the nations. Pass the *charoses*, please"—spans hours and hours.

In fact, much of the Haggadah could seemingly benefit from a discerning editor keen on eliminating apparent repetition. *Dayeinu* could be truncated. *Echad Mi Yodei'a* could be streamlined. Even *Chad Gadya* could fast-forward to the final stanza and we'd all be wrapping up quite a bit earlier.

But that never happens. To the contrary. We relish the details. It brings the night to life. It brings the past to the present and illuminates our future. Every step of *Dayeinu* deserves a praise to Hashem. Every digit (up to twelve) gets its own stanza. And even the stick, fire, water, and ox get their own cameo appearance.

At the Seder, it's the details that bring the night to life.

As Van der Rohe said, "G-d is in the detail." On this triumphant night, when Yidden the world over celebrate the priceless opportunity to serve as Hashem's nation, may we merit to bring the details to life in a vibrant way that leaves an indelible impression on all of the night's participants—and most of all, ourselves.

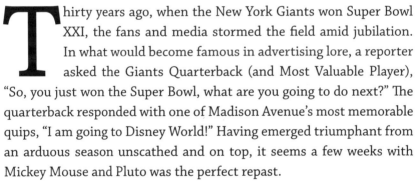

Shevi'i Shel Pesach

Post-Pharaoh Perspectives

T hirty years ago, when the New York Giants won Super Bowl XXI, the fans and media stormed the field amid jubilation. In what would become famous in advertising lore, a reporter asked the Giants Quarterback (and Most Valuable Player), "So, you just won the Super Bowl, what are you going to do next?" The quarterback responded with one of Madison Avenue's most memorable quips, "I am going to Disney World!" Having emerged triumphant from an arduous season unscathed and on top, it seems a few weeks with Mickey Mouse and Pluto was the perfect repast.

The Torah, viewed through the lenses of Chazal, provides a glimpse of where our sights should be set in a post-Pharaoh world. And—no surprise—it's less expensive, less crowded, and less Goofy than Disney World.

Among all the myriad subjects discussed throughout the 2,700-plus pages of Talmud, we find numerous occasions where our Sages opine as to who has a place in the Next World. Rav Yochanan, for instance, asked "Who is a *ben Olam Haba* (has a place in the Next World)? Anyone who connects *geulah* (mention of the redemption from Egypt) to *tefillah* during *Maariv*."[118]

The knee-jerk reaction (which is presumably irking you right now) is addressed by none less than Rabbeinu Yonah, who writes, "Just because one 'connects *geulah* to *tefillah*' is he worthy of being a *ben Olam Haba*?" That doesn't seem too difficult. Much less expensive than eating kosher. Much less taxing than cleaning for Pesach. Much less time-consuming than mastering the Torah. Much less frustrating than actually trying to get along with others. That's it?! Just choreograph my davening such that I don't space out between *geulah* and *tefillah*, resist the urge to text my wife (again) in the middle of davening, and I can book my ticket for the Next World?! What's the big deal?

Rabbeinu Yonah explains that the recognition of our nation's miraculous redemption from Egypt infuses our *tefillos* with a heightened degree of *bitachon* and a keener awareness of Hashem's limitless capacity to fulfill any lack (real or perceived) in one's life. Be it health, wealth, brains, peace (on a global scale or simply with one's spouse—not sure which is more realistic), *nachas* (or nachos, if you don't have enough), a traffic-free commute, or an uninterrupted Shabbos nap. Bottom line, there is simply no such thing as a Mission Impossible in Hashem's Divine playbook.

"Yisrael saw the great hand that Hashem inflicted upon Egypt; and the people revered Hashem and they *had faith* in Hashem."[119] Not just then, but for all time. When we recall our triumphant and improbable liberation from Mitzrayim—a promise that Hashem delivered on in spades—we have access to a true streak of *bitachon* that yes, Hashem will similarly hearken unto *my* personal plea, even those that seem remote and far gone.

> The trick is to bring the *emunah* of the Exodus into the *emunah* of the everyday.

Fine. That bodes well for my own personal *tefillah*, but how exactly does that become the recipe for

---

118 *Berachos* 4b.
119 *Shemos* 14:31.

Olam Haba? Rabbeinu Yonah posits that the octane that fuels a Yid's *avodas Hashem* is none other than *bitachon*. Accordingly, the synergy that is created when one hearkens back to Mitzrayim and *immediately* endeavors to bring the *emunah* of the Exodus into the *emunah* of the everyday; such is the catalyst that can kindle all the various facets of our *avodas Hashem*. Empowered with this *emunah*, one is equipped to live a life worthy of a fifty-yard-line seat in the Next World.

In this respect, the culmination of the Plagues, the downfall of Pharaoh, and the long-awaited redemption of Am Yisrael constitute *both* ancient history and current events. May we merit to seize the opportunity to strengthen our own *emunah* and thereby pave the way for all the *yeshuos* that all Yidden seek, *b'klal u'b'prat*.

Shavuos

Leap of Love

The ability to ride a bike is one of the most liberating experiences of a child's early years. Invariably, however, it is preceded by an array of spills and scratches, falls and boo-boos, until one can muster the requisite coordination of balance, strength, and pedaling. Early in my own post-training-wheel era, I recall my hesitation to ride on the pavement, preferring instead to stick to natural surfaces (i.e., the grass) such that a sudden wipe-out would land me on the cushy ground instead of the less-forgiving asphalt.

That remained my comfort zone until my father pointed out that—notwithstanding the risks involved—riding on the driveway was *really* the way to go and would be advantageous in many respects: a smoother terrain, a swifter (albeit manageable) pace, and ultimately, the surface that would enable me to get the "hang of the whole thing" more easily and successfully. Lo and behold, I put my trust in my dad's assessment and voilà, before you knew it, I was off and running (or pedaling, as the case may be).

And [Am Yisrael] said, "We will do and we will listen!"[120]

---

120 *Shemos* 23:7.

With this singular expression of ultimate dedication, Klal Yisrael's unconditional commitment to Hashem was minted. An eternal relationship was forged—one whose anniversary we celebrate on Shavuos night.

As the Talmud recounts, a certain cynic took exception to this famous declaration, claiming: "You are an impetuous people, for you put your mouth before your ears [saying that you would *do* before you even knew what the commandments would be.]"[121]

Lest we be accused of rashly racing into a relationship of unknown parameters (with eternity on the line), perhaps we can view our ancestors' national en masse decision to accept the Torah sight unseen, lock, stock, and barrel, as the logical, rational extension of their deep-seated love and trust in Hashem. Their loving, compassionate Father in whom they could completely rely that whatever He had in store for them was undoubtedly in their best interest. That whatever the Torah contained would be tailor-made for their ultimate good (spiritual, physical, emotional, etc.) and conducive to a life of meaningfulness and deep-seated satisfaction.

To be sure, trusting in that relationship did not happen overnight. To the contrary, it began in Mitzrayim and reached an apex the night of Pesach. After that, Am Yisrael experienced forty-nine days of *temimus* within which to contemplate Hashem's greatness and internalize His paternal desire to direct His limitless wisdom and might for the well-being of His beloved Yidden. Infused with forty-nine days of awareness of Hashem's goodness, the willing acceptance of the Torah—sight unseen—could nevertheless be both genuine and wholehearted. How? Because that commitment was rendered on the basis of our trust in Hashem as a Loving Father. Viewed in this light, our acceptance of the Torah was not so much a "leap of faith" as it was a "leap of love."

Our acceptance of the Torah was not so much a "leap of faith" as it was a "leap of love."

Our *avodah* on Shavuos is more than just our renewed acceptance and commitment to the Torah, the keeping thereof

---

121 *Shabbos* 88a–b.

and the learning thereof. Beyond that, we have an amazing opportunity to renew our commitment to Hashem Himself.

In sum, perhaps that is why a Jew makes two separate *berachos* on the Torah each and every morning. Why doesn't one suffice (as it does with virtually every other mitzvah from matzah to mezuzah)? In light of the above, perhaps the first blessing applies to the Torah itself (and the recognition of our obligation to be *oseik* in its words and dictates). The second blessing, however, transcends the Torah itself and is uttered in deep-seated appreciation for the *relationship* that we merit to have with Hashem who, via Har Sinai, "chose us from among the nations and gave us His Torah."

> On Shavuos, we celebrate not only our acceptance of the Torah, but the relationship we entered into on account of this acceptance.

As we prepare ourselves—individually and collectively—to march down to our national *chuppah* and to renew our dedication to the Torah, may we all merit to feel the sweetness and fulfillment associated with having a deep and meaningful relationship with the *Borei Olam*. A relationship that was forged three thousand-plus years ago at the foot of Har Sinai.

Tishah B'Av

A Daughter's Wish

T he following encounter occurred when my mother was davening at the Kosel. While the Kosel has an otherworldliness to it that inexplicably creates a sense of peace and privacy with Hashem, it was virtually impossible not to notice a younger girl (perhaps not more than thirteen years of age) who was davening in close proximity. Apparently, this young woman offered a *Shemoneh Esrei* that spanned nearly thirty minutes, most of which was accompanied by heartfelt cries and heartrending tears. This thirteen-year-old had just sobbed through the very davening that many of us may find dry.

At the conclusion of their respective *tefillos*, my mom politely inquired (without prying) if there was anything she could do. Who knew what lay at the root of this young girl's tears? Perhaps her mother was battling an illness. Perhaps her father had lost his job. Perhaps there was a name that could be davened for. Perhaps some words of *chizuk* and comfort would buoy the young girl's spirits.

In response, the young girl looked up and said, "Thank you so much. That's very kind. *Baruch Hashem*. It's fine. Today is my birthday and I'm davening to Hashem that He rebuild His Beis Hamikdash." And daven she did, with all her heart and flowing tears.

A thirty-minute heartfelt prayer! And what lay at the heart of her yearning? Yerushalayim. Rather than a plea for a new bicycle, sticker collection, or diary, first and foremost in this girl's heart was a prayer for Hashem's Home. Not just a bunk bed or a new pair of shoes. Uncluttered by visions of accumulating more things and detached from the allure of more ephemeral pleasures, this young girl of uncommon maturity tapped into a painful reality that most of us routinely overlook (albeit not deliberately).

"It's my birthday and I'm davening for Hashem to restore His Beis Hamikdash."

She tapped into a reality that the Kosel brings home—that notwithstanding our mission of being a light unto the nations (and the many respects in which we've accomplished that mission) and our sincere pursuit of wisdom (and the thousands who joyfully endure all types of self-sacrifice to accumulate such wisdom) and our *chessed* (much of which will never be known to others)—Hashem's abode on earth still remains in ruins, and Yerushalayim still beckons to be rebuilt.

May this year be the one where the tears of this young girl run together with the centuries of Jewish tears and usher in an "*ohr chadash al Tzion*—a new light in Zion."

Rosh Hashanah

Tipping the Scales

iants Stadium seems to be an unlikely venue from which to glean Torah insights. Anyway, facing fourth down and a yard to go, the hometown Giants brought out their punting squad. Anticipating a seemingly ho-hum, insignificant, routine punt, thousands of fans flocked en masse to the concession stands, seeking (more) beer and (more) hot dogs.

However, amid that stampede, word quickly caught on that the Giants had yanked the punting unit *off* the field and the offense was back in there. Yes, they were "going to go for it." "They're going for it?" queried Giants fans. "Yup...they're going for it!" Like a hot stock tip, the word passed like wildfire, "THEY'RE GOING FOR IT!" And with those magical words, thousands instantly forgot their thirst, disregarded their appetite, stopped in their tracks, and were now roaring at the top of their lungs. "Goooooo!" What happened, I confess, I don't recall. Was the play a success or a bust? I have no clue. What did stick with me is the notion that *one* coach made *one* decision that brought 82,000-plus-fans to their feet with excitement and fervor.

Life, at its core, is merely one decision after another. As humans, we are blessed with the unique power of "choice" and the capacity to exercise free will. That being said, routines set in, patterns are established, and deep, meaningful, macro-level, game-changing decisions are seemingly few and far between. This reality makes life predictable and provides a stable framework within which to spend our days. Predictable, however, is not always profitable.

When one opts to "go for it," who knows what commotion is stirred in the Heavens?

Don't underestimate the spiritual "wind in your sails." For when a Jew decides that he or she is going to "go for it," who knows what commotion is stirred in the Heavens? Not to punt on our dreams and ambitions, but rather to take affirmative steps toward fulfilling our individual and communal destiny.

A decision to take one's observance to the next level. One's mitzvos. One's Torah learning. One's davening. One's marriage. One's character. One's *emunah*. One's care and concern for others. One's relationship with Hashem. Make that extra minyan. Do that extra *chessed*. Go that extra mile.

If you have the courage to push yourself forward, to push yourself out of the comfort zone of inertia, listen, and perhaps, in the quiet recesses of your mind, you might even hear the uproar emanating from *Shamayim* as thousands of the Heavenly angels resound in support of your decision to "go for it!"

If you listen further, you might even hear the Divine scales tipping in your favor. Or in Am Yisrael's favor. One choice. One firm commitment. One proactive, positive change in the right direction. It could just be the very decision that will tip the scales for a life full of happiness, peace, prosperity, and fulfillment.

Yom Kippur

Pardon Our Appearance

Imagine a handyman who diligently waits for potential clients to enlist his services. *Ring-ring.* "Mr. Handyman. I am in the last legs of renovation and all that needs to be done is to install a few wall hangings. A couple of photos. A painting. A mirror or two. Can you help with that?"

True, thinks the handyman, *this project doesn't sound like heavy lifting, but how lucrative could it be? An hour? Two hours tops. Barely seems worth it.*

Ring-ring. "Mr. Handyman. It's Governor Cuomo. I have an airport here, known as LaGuardia, which is 'now an outdated and poorly designed complex.' I have a vision to essentially gut the whole thing and replace it 'with the world-class airport New York has always deserved.' Let's face it—as airports go, it's essentially a third-world set-up. Traffic is a disaster. Parking virtually nonexistent. Infrastructure crumbling. But with your help and extensive renovations from the ground up, we can really accomplish something major and lasting."

True, thinks the handyman, *this project could tie me up for several years, but think how lucrative it could be!*

Having undertaken a thorough once-over, a *cheshbon ha'nefesh* (self-accounting) of where we are and where we should be, let's face it...can any of us confidently say we have our name indelibly inked in the *Sefer HaChaim* at this point? We're all teetering on the brink, and—let me speak for myself, at least—when held up to the glaring light of objectivity, glaring gaps in our spiritual portfolio are readily discernible. Concentration in davening needs revamping. Commitment to Torah learning needs rejuvenation. Mitzvos need to be reinvigorated lest they become (even more) rote. Shabbos needs an upgrade. And that's just between us and Hashem.

What about our *middos* and interactions with others? They also present no shortage of yellow (and perhaps red) flags. Arrogance. Impatience. Self-centeredness. Jealousy. Ingratitude. Argumentativeness.

What about our own personal foibles and flaws? Laziness. Anxiety. Negativity. Inability to appreciate that which is good in our lives.

In short, to whatever degree it may be—major renovations are surely in order.

Alas, Hashem, in His abundant kindness, grants us a Yom Kippur. A day when we can be real with ourselves, with all our imperfections (those we were born with and those we acquired along the way); to acknowledge them, embrace them, and humbly beseech Hashem, "Please pardon our appearance while we undergo extensive renovations."

> The first steps in fixing oneself are the self-awareness of what needs to be fixed and the commitment to undertake personal renovations.

For the first step in fixing is realizing what needs to be fixed. And the fixing itself—well, that's the very endeavor we are expected to dedicate our life's efforts toward. Our portion in *Olam Haba* will directly reflect the degree to which we worked on renovating ourselves during our stint in *Olam Hazeh*.

So many people live with the (mistaken) notion that Yom Kippur is a sad, sober sequel to Tishah b'Av. Quite the contrary. Rabbi Mayer Birnbaum writes that during the Yom Kippur *Amidah*, "one should feel tremendous gratitude toward the Almighty for the *gift* of Yom Kippur, the day on which He forgives our sins, if we repent" (emphasis supplied).

Similarly, the *Yesod V'Shoresh Ha'avodah* writes that when one utters the *She'hechiyanu* that ushers in the rarefied *kedushah* of Yom Kippur, one should do so with "abundant joyfulness and gratitude toward Hashem for enabling" one to experience another Yom Kippur and fulfill the mitzvos of the day (i.e., fasting, *davening*, and *teshuvah*).

May we merit to rise to the once-a-year opportunity of Yom Kippur. To meet our flaws head-on and begin tackling them with Divine assistance. May Hashem mercifully keep the Gates of *Teshuvah* open for each and every Jewish *neshamah*, and may we *all* be written into *all* the good books for a year of health, prosperity, and *chayim tovim*, and may Hashem deal with us with *tzedakah* and *chessed*.

Sukkos

The Simchah of "Significance"

Of all our festivals, Sukkos is the most diverse and multidimensional. Whereas the various mitzvos of Pesach, (e.g., matzah, the four cups of wine, the *maror*, the chametz-free existence) all stem from the overarching celebration of our national liberation from Mitzrayim, it's harder to discern a common thread linking the seemingly disparate mitzvos of Sukkos. What is the common denominator uniting (a) the sukkah, (b) the *arbah minim*, (c) the *nisuch ha'mayim* (water-offering ceremony), and (d) the reading of *Koheles*? Obviously, on some macro level they each contribute to the personal and national joyousness of *zman simchaseinu*, but how?

Decades ago, the South African De Beers Mines launched an ad campaign boldly proclaiming that "diamonds are forever." Perhaps Sukkos teaches us that diamonds aren't the *only* substance that is forever. Rather, within the Torah's matrix, an esrog can be forever, twigs can be forever, and yes, even water is forever. Let's see how.

Joy is the by-product of meaningfulness.

In a wide variety of contexts, the extent of one's joy is directly related to the meaningfulness of what a person is involved in. For instance,

194

in 1951, Bobby Thomson's ninth-inning, game-winning homerun won the pennant for the New York Giants (aka "the shot heard round the world"). Now, consider that Thomson hit 263 other homeruns over a fourteen-year career. I venture he probably hit countless more in high school and practice. But if we'd ask him, "Hey, Bobby, which of those was most memorable? Which round-tripper produced the greatest degree of happiness?" Would any of them even remotely compare to the one that won the pennant? Not by a long shot. That one was historic. That one assured his place in the annals of baseball history. That one took on an exponentially greater significance—one that would transcend time and place and achieve a rare degree of lastingness. Children would relive that moment for generations to come.

Along these lines, the mitzvos of Sukkos each echo a similar sentiment—namely, that a Jew can achieve truly great and immortal significance merely by adhering to the Torah and its timeless wisdom. And more than that, one can do so with the most seemingly mundane and insignificant raw materials. The Torah instructs us to construct the sukkah's rickety roof with the "leftovers" from the harvest. Discarded twigs and otherwise useless vines. The esrog, lulav, *hadassim*, and *aravos* hardly have any usefulness outside of the week of Sukkos. Their sole "claim to fame" is the mitzvah to take them once a year on the fifteenth of Tishrei (the Rabbis later instituted to take them throughout the festival). Water? What could be more insignificant and ho-hum than water? Tasteless. Colorless. Abundantly in supply. Doesn't even provide nourishment. And yet, its placement on the *Mizbei'ach* served as a catalyst for the greatest display of *simchah* that the Talmud ever records. For even water—under the right circumstances—can serve as a conduit for a connection to the Eternal.

Koheles, too, amplifies this theme that virtually every facet of life—travel, cuisine, wealth, whatever it may be—is capable of immense intrinsic and eternal meaningfulness when engaged through the lenses of the Torah and viewed as a component of one's *avodas Hashem*.

In short, with the Torah as one's guide, the most mundane has the capacity for timelessness. The most ho-hum has the potential for greatness. If we saturate ourselves with this notion—via the sukkah's roof, via the *arba minim*, via the *nisuch ha'mayim*, and via *Koheles*—we can equip ourselves with the capacity to infuse true meaningfulness into virtually every encounter of our lives. And when our days become transformed from the ordinary into the extraordinary, so too will we discover the recipe for true happiness.

Shemini Atzeres

Go Ahead...
Make
My Day

S aying good-bye to someone, be it with profundity or perfunctorily, is often just about taking leave of one another in a socially acceptable fashion. Appropriate salutations are offered. Well-wishes are conveyed. And each party is off to the next. Life rolls on. People to see. Places to go.

Saying good-bye to our festivals, however, is an altogether different art form and one which demands forethought lest the odyssey fizzle out upon reentry into the orbit of everyday life. Take Pesach, for instance, where the wise son at the table is instructed regarding "the laws of the Pesach offering" and, in particular, "that one may not eat dessert after the final taste of the Pesach offering."[122] Even if he ate a *really* good supper, there's nothing to be consumed after the afikomen—for doing so might would torpedo the whole leave-taking of the Seder.

What the matzah lacks in tastiness it more than makes up for in meaningfulness. Hence, the mandate to let that taste (or lack thereof) linger. No more *kosher l'Pesach* candy. Rein in that desire for another

---

122   Pesach Haggadah.

macaroon. Rather, give bandwidth to all the matzah's connotations of oppression and freedom and faithfulness and eternity and let them breathe, so to speak (like a recently uncorked savory wine). Be sure not to curtail its impact by ingesting another piece of almond bark. *That's the way to say a proper farewell to the Pesach Seder.*

Great. But what about Sukkos? How do we take leave of the spiritual voyage that we have collectively experienced in the twenty-five days that have unfolded since Rosh Hashanah? How does the shofar still resonate in our ears? How does Yom Kippur still stick to our souls? How does Sukkos remain in the post lulav-shaking, *aravos*-beating, sukkah-dwelling, *ushpizin*-inviting, Torah-dancing world?

One answer, perhaps, lies in the worldview that we have hopefully adopted during these rarefied days. A view of joy and positivity. A view of appreciation and purposefulness.

How many times did we proclaim, "Give thanks to Hashem for He is good, His kindness endures forever"?[123] With the esrog. Without the esrog. Juggling the siddur. Impaling the guy davening in front of you. Again and again and again and again. Sometimes slower. Sometimes louder. Sometimes feeling it to our core and other times wondering what's for breakfast.

How many times did we express our conviction that Hashem's "kindness endures forever"?

How many times did we thank Hashem, *she'hechiyanu v'kiyimanu v'higiyanu la'zman ha'zeh*, for the pleasure and privilege of reaching another milestone in life? By my count, at least ten times in the first few weeks of the calendar year (twice on Rosh Hashanah, twice before shofar blowing, once on Yom Kippur, twice on Sukkos, once before taking the lulav, and twice more on Shemini Atzeres).

How many times did we exuberantly dance around and around our respective shuls with the Torah during Simchas Torah? And not just with *your* shul. But if you put your mind and heart to it you can hear other shuls—down the block, in Boro Park, in Toronto, in Gateshead,

---

123 *Tehillim* 136.

in Sydney...the world over, one can hear the pure joyfulness and appreciation of being included among Am Yisrael, bellowing forth into the Yom Tov night sky.

More than that, if you *really* put your mind and heart to it, you can envision yourself dancing with the Chafetz Chaim in Radin in the 1930s or the Netziv in Volozhin in the 1860s, or the Chasam Sofer in Pressburg in the 1820s. For your dancing and singing became yet another refrain in the endless joy of Simchas Torah that has survived every anti-Torah and every anti-*simchah* obstacle in the long gauntlet of exile.

In short, the national (and personal) metamorphosis during the month of Tishrei culminates in a crescendo of pure *simchah* and appreciation that *you* have been tapped as a torchbearer of the Torah and a member of Am Yisrael. That unique perspective on life is crystallized with the reading (in rapid succession) of *parashas Bereishis*, wherein we hear again and again how each and every facet of the Creation was "*tov.*" The light.[124] The earth and seas.[125] The vast plant kingdom, including teeming numbers of trees, vegetation, and fruits.[126] The sun and moon.[127] So on and so forth. "And G-d saw all that He had made, and behold it was *very good.*"[128]

When the dust settles on Sukkos, we are left with the culmination of the *Chumash*'s final words, "Before the eyes of all Israel"[129] and the immediate juxtaposition of the *Chumash*'s first words, "In the beginning of Hashem's creating the heavens and the earth."[130] The sentiment is (hopefully) clear that "the eyes of all Israel" are uniquely equipped (and expected) to perceive Hashem's Divine Hand (and Wisdom and Kindliness) throughout this very good world.

> The "eyes" of Yisrael are uniquely equipped and expected to perceive Hashem throughout His very good world.

---

124   *Bereishis* 1:4.
125   Ibid. 1:9.
126   Ibid. 1:12.
127   Ibid. 1:18.
128   Ibid. 1:31.
129   *Devarim* 34:12.
130   *Bereishis* 1:1.

We have said farewell to the sukkah. The decorations will soon be stashed away until next year. The leftovers will soon be consumed. The sore knees and hoarse voices will soon (hopefully) be back to full vigor. What will we be left with? As we said in *Hallel* so many times, the empowering recognition that "this is the day Hashem has made" and the amazing opportunity to "let us rejoice and be glad on it."[131]

May we be successful in doing so and may we merit to see all that is good, day in and day out, in Hashem's very good world. *L'shanah ha'baah b'Yerushalayim*, next year in Jerusalem.

---

131   *Tehillim* 118:24.

Conclusion

"**I**t is worthwhile," Rabbi Yisroel Salanter said, "to give a lengthy *mussar* discourse if all it accomplishes is that one person will pray one prayer with *kavanah*…even if that one person is myself." In a similar vein, this project will have been worthwhile if just one reader musters the latent wherewithal to deepen his or her relationship with Hashem and refine their capacity to perceive His goodness in this world. If it produces another ounce of *simchas ha'chayim* in the world, the *sefer*, I believe, has been justified.

That being said, I ask just one last word against that naysaying voice within saying, "Yeah, but those types of things *never* happen to me." To that streak of self-doubt, I offer the following words from, of all places, Freddie Patek, an infielder for the Kansas City Royals (among other squads) who had the somewhat dubious honor of being the shortest player in professional baseball in his day. When he broke into the Major Leagues, some insensitive reporter asked, "So, Freddie, how does it feel to be the *shortest* player in the major leagues?" Unfazed, Freddie responded, "Well, it's sure better than being the *tallest* player in the minors!"

We thank Hashem every morning "for separating us from those who go astray." From the masses of humanity that are completely oblivious to Hashem's existence and entirely indifferent to His Wisdom and Kindness that render every day an opportunity to sing with gratitude and happiness. Would we prefer a different lot in life? Perhaps. Could things be better? We like to think so. Should that rob *you* of *your* unique capacity to seize *your* moments and live fully? For sure not.

Strive. Seek. Don't give up. Don't give in. Today awaits you. What greatness will you find in it? What insights will you inscribe on it?

May we embrace the day that Hashem has blessed us with.

May we merit to seize the moments and their meaningfulness.

May the meaningfulness of our days generate true *simchas ha'chayim*.

May we harness that *simchas ha'chayim* to enable others to taste the sweetness of a purposeful life.

And may we soon celebrate that Great Day[132] when Hashem will restore His Shechinah to Tzion—may it be speedily in our days, amen.

---

132 *Malachi* 3:23.

Glossary

adam gadol: A person who exemplifies greatness of character.

ahavas chessed: Love of kindness.

ahavas Yisrael: Love for other Jews.

eishes chayil: Woman of valor.

Am Yisrael: A reference to the Jewish People at large.

Amidah: The central prayer in the daily prayer service.

arba minim: The Four Species taken on Sukkos.

Aron: The Holy Ark that housed the Tablets (*Luchos*).

Av Ha'rachamim: Lit., Merciful Father.

aveirah (pl.–aveiros): Sin(s); transgression(s).

Avinu She'baShamayim: Our Father in Heaven.

avodah: Service to Hashem.

avodas ha'kodesh: Holy service.

avodas Hashem: Service of Hashem.

Avraham Avinu: Our forefather Abraham.

baal teshuvah: Person who returns to Torah observance.

bar mitzvah: Celebration when a Jewish male reaches the age of thirteen and becomes obligated in the commandments.

baruch Hashem: Lit., blessed is Hashem; thank Hashem; an expression of Hashem's goodness.

bashert: Soul mate.

bayis: Home.

bedeken: The veiling ceremony prior to a Jewish wedding.

beis midrash: Torah study hall.

Beis Hamikdash: Holy Temple in Jerusalem.

Beis Yisrael: House of Israel.

berachah: Blessing.

Bereishis: Book of Genesis.

bikur cholim: Lit., visiting the sick.

bimah: Lectern.

binah: Insight.

bitachon: Trust in G-d.

Borei Olam: Creator of the World.

bubbies: (Yiddish) Grandmothers.

b'klal u'b'prat: In general and specifically.

chochmah: Wisdom.

chametz: Leavened foods prohibited during the Passover festival.

charoses: A mixture into which the *maror* is dipped at the Passover Seder. Made of wine, nuts, apples, and cinnamon, its color and consistency are meant to remind us of the bricks and mortar used by the Jewish slaves in Egypt.

chassid: Jew associated with a particular Chassidic sect.

Chavah: Eve.

chayim tovim: Good life.

Chazal: The Sages, of blessed memory.

Cheit Ha'eigel: Sin of the Golden Calf.

chessed: Loving-kindness.

chinuch: Education; training.

chizuk: Encouragement.

chochmas haTorah: Torah wisdom.

cholent: Hearty meat stew traditionally served on the Sabbath.

Chovos HaLevavos: Lit., "Duties of the Heart," written by Rabbeinu Bachya ibn Pakuda in eleventh-century Spain.

Chumash: The Five Books of the Torah.

chuppah: Wedding canopy.

daas Torah: True comprehension based on Torah knowledge.

daven: Pray.

Dayeinu: Section of Passover Seder that praises Hashem for the kindnesses He bestowed upon the Jewish Nation.

derech ha'mussar: Behavior in accord with the Torah's notion of morality and ethical conduct.

divrei chizuk: Words of encouragement.

derashah: Sermon.

emes: Truth.

emunah: Faith; belief in G-d; faithfulness.

erev Shabbos: Friday afternoon before the onset of the Sabbath.

Eretz Yisrael: Land of Israel.

eved Hashem (pl.–ovdei Hashem): Servant(s) of G-d.

fleishig: (Yiddish) Meaty.

gadol ha'dor: Torah leader of the generation.

Gan Eden: Garden of Eden.

geshmak: (Yiddish) Delicious; delightful.

Haggadah: Liturgy recited at the Passover Seder.

hakafah: Dance around the synagogue during the holiday of Simchas Torah.

Hallel: Lit., praise; a prayer of praise and thanksgiving recited during prayer services on Rosh Chodesh and most festivals, and in the Haggadah.

hanhalah: Faculty.

hakaras ha'tov: Gratitude; Expressing gratitude.

Har Sinai: Mount Sinai.

hashgachah pratis: Divine providence.

Hashem: G-d.

Havdalah: Ritual performed at conclusion of the Sabbath or festival demarcating between the holy and the profane.

Kaddish: Prayer recited regularly during prayer service.

kanfei Shechinah: The wings of the Divine Presence.

kavanah: Concentration.

kedushah: Holiness.

ketores: The incense offered in the Beis Hamikdash.

kever: Grave.

Keruvim: Angelic beings, golden depictions of which sat atop the Holy Ark in the Holy Temple.

Kiddush: Blessing over wine made on Friday night to sanctify the Sabbath.

kiddush Hashem: Doing something that brings honor to Hashem; sanctification of G-d's Name.

kippah serugah: Knitted yarmulke.

Klal Yisrael: The Jewish People.

kochos: Strengths.

Koheles: Book of Ecclesiastes written by King Solomon.

Kohen (pl.–Kohanim): Priest(s), direct male descendant(s) of Aharon, brother of Moshe.

Kohen Gadol: The High Priest who served in the Beis Hamikdash.

Kol Nidrei: The opening prayer service of Yom Kippur.

korban (pl.–korbanos): Sacrificial offering(s).

Kosel: Western Wall in Jerusalem; the Wailing Wall.

kvetching: (Yiddish) Complaining.

L'hadlik Ner: Blessing on lighting of candles.

limud haTorah: Study of the Torah.

Litvaks: Jews hailing from Lithuanian descent.

lashon hara: Lit., evil speech; derogatory, slanderous, or harmful speech; gossip.

Maariv: Evening prayer service.

machlokes: An argument; dispute.

machatzis ha'shekel: Half-shekel coin.

ma'amin: Believer.

marbitz Torah: Disseminator of Torah wisdom.

mazel tov: Lit., good fortune; an expression of congratulations.

Me'aras HaMachpeilah: Burial cave in Chevron of Abraham and Sarah, Isaac and Rivkah, and Jacob and Leah.

mechanech: Educator.

megillah: Scroll; usually refers to the Book of Esther, which describes the story of the Purim miracle.

mekadesh: Sanctify.

Menachos: Tractate of the Talmud pertaining to grain offerings.

Menorah: Seven-branched candelabrum in the Holy Temple.

mensch: (Yiddish) Person of integrity and honor.

menschlichkeit: (Yiddish) Acting with integrity and honor.

menuchah: Rest; peace of mind.

menuchas ha'nefesh: Peace of mind; spiritual calm.

mesirus nefesh: Self-sacrifice; selfless devotion.

mesorah: Jewish tradition transmitted from one generation to the next.

metzora: One afflicted with the skin disease *tzaraas*.

mezuzah: Small parchment scroll in a casing, affixed to a doorpost and containing the first two paragraphs of the *Shema* prayer.

middah (pl.–middos): Character trait(s).

milchig: (Yiddish) Dairy.

minyan: Quorum of ten adult Jewish men needed for public prayer service.

Mishkan: Tabernacle; the portable Temple used by Jews during their sojourn in the Wilderness.

Mishnah: Basic codification of the Oral Torah assembled by Rabbi Yehudah HaNasi in the third century.

mishpachah: Family.

Mitzrayim: Egypt.

mitzvah (pl.–mitzvos): Torah commandment(s).

Mizbei'ach: Sacrificial altar.

morah: Teacher.

Moshe Rabbeinu: Moses, our teacher.

Mussaf: Supplementary prayer service added to the Sabbath and festival morning services.

mussar: Character improvement.

nachas: Deep-seated sense of satisfaction.

navi: Prophet.

nechamah: Consolation.

Ne'ilah: Concluding prayer of Yom Kippur.

ner Chanukah: Chanukah light or candle.

ner (pl.–neiros): Candle(s).

neshamah (pl.–neshamos): Soul(s).

nosh: Snacks.

olah: Type of sacrifice that is totally burned on the Altar.

Olam Haba: The World to Come; the afterlife.

Olam Hazeh: This world.

Orchos Tzaddikim: Lit., "Paths of the Righteous," anonymously authored fifteenth-century classic work on ethical conduct.

parashah (pl.–parashiyos): Weekly Torah portion(s).

pashut: Simple.

Pirkei Avos: Lit., "Chapters of the Fathers," the Mishnaic tractate that focuses on moral and ethical teachings.

poskim: Authorities in halachah (Jewish law).

Rabbeinu Bachya: Thirteenth-century Torah commentator.

rachamim: Mercy.

Ramban: Rabbi Moshe ben Nachman, also known as Nachmanides, a famous twelfth-century rabbi.

Rashi: Eleventh-century French rabbi, considered the "father of all Torah commentators."

rav: Rabbi.

rebbeim: Torah teachers.

rebbetzin: Title given to the wife of a rabbi.

Rosh Chodesh: First day of the Jewish month.

Rosh Yeshiva (pl.–roshei yeshiva): Head(s) or dean(s) of Torah schools.

sefer (pl.–sefarim): Book(s).

Sefer HaChaim: Book of Life.

Sefer Torah: Torah scroll.

Shaar Ha'bitachon: The section of *Chovos HaLevavos* that explains what it means to trust in Hashem.

shaatnez: Mixture of wool and linen, prohibited by Torah law.

Shabbos: The Sabbath.

Shacharis: Morning prayer.

shadchan (pl.–shadchanim): Matchmaker(s).

shalom: Peace.

Shalom aleichem: Lit., "Peace be upon you," often said on meeting or leave-taking.

shalom bayis: Marital harmony.

Shamayim: Heaven.

She'asah Nissim: Blessing praising the miracles Hashem performed for the Jewish People.

shekel: Type of coin mentioned in the Torah.

Shema: Declaration of our allegiance to Hashem expressed in three paragraphs of the Torah that are recited twice daily.

Shemoneh Esrei: Lit., eighteen; the central prayer that is the core of each weekday prayer service.

shevet: Tribe.

shemiras ha'lashon: Laws governing proper speech.

Shemos: Book of Exodus.

shidduch (pl.–shidduchim): Marriage-match(es).

Shir HaShirim: Lit., "Song of Songs," composed by King Solomon.

shivah: Week-long mourning period following the loss of a close relative.

shleimus: Completion.

shlita: Hebrew acronym for "May he live a length of good days, Amen."

shomer Shabbos: Someone who safeguards the Sabbath by keeping its laws.

shtreimel: (Yiddish) Traditional hat worn by Chassidim on Sabbath and festivals.

shul: Synagogue.

Shulchan: The Golden Table in the Holy Temple.

simchah: Happiness; a happy occasion.

simchas ha'chayim: Joy of life.

Simchas Torah: Jewish holiday celebrating the annual completion of the Torah, celebrated with much fanfare, singing, and dancing.

sinas chinam: Baseless hatred; alienation or estrangement among Jews.

sukkah: Booth in which Jews are commanded to dwell during the festival of Sukkos

taharah: Spiritual purity.

talmid chacham (pl.–talmidei chachamim): Lit., the student of a wise person; Torah scholar; accomplished Torah scholar; a person learned in Torah and Talmud.

talmid (pl.–talmidim): Student(s).

Talmud: Compilation of the Oral Law.

temimus: Wholesomeness.

Tanach: Acronym for Torah, *Nevi'im*, and *Kesuvim*; the written Torah, including the Five Books of Moses, the eight books of Prophets, and the eleven books of Writings.

tefillah (pl.–tefillos): Prayer(s).

tefillin: Phylacteries; small black leather boxes containing parchment scrolls inscribed with Biblical passages, worn on the arm and head by adult Jewish males during the weekday morning prayer service.

Tehillim: Psalms.

teshuvah: Repentance and return to the way of life prescribed by the Torah.

Tishah b'Av: The ninth day of the month of Av, a day of national mourning for the destruction of the Holy Temples in Jerusalem.

Tishrei: Month in the Jewish calendar when Rosh Hashanah, Yom Kippur, and Sukkos occur.

Totty: (Yiddish) Father.

treif: Colloquial term for nonkosher.

tzaraas: A severe (spiritual) skin affliction that manifests (on people) as white or light-colored spots on the body.

tzedakah: Charity.

tzniyus: Modesty.

tzaros: (Yiddish) Trials and tribulations; suffering.

Yerushalayim: Jerusalem.

yeshiva: Educational institution dedicated to the study of Torah.

yeshuos: Salvations.

yetzias Mitzrayim: The Exodus from Egypt.

Yid (pl.–Yidden): (Yiddish) Jew(s).

Yiddishkeit: Judaism; the Jewish way of life.

Yom Tov: Jewish festival.

zeidy: (Yiddish) Grandfather.

zman simchaseinu: The time of our joyfulness.

zt"l: Acronym for "*zecher tzaddik livrachah*—may the memory of the righteous be blessed."

About
the Author

Rabbi Yered Michoel (a.k.a. Jared) Viders hails from Huntington, New York. Upon his graduation from law school, he learned Torah in Jerusalem. After returning to America, Rabbi Viders served as a judicial law clerk on the highest court in the Commonwealth of Massachusetts. He then moved to Monsey, New York, to continue learning in Yeshiva Ohr Somayach.

Currently, in addition to practicing law, Rabbi Viders teaches at Ohr Somayach Monsey. As outreach coordinator for JEP of Westchester, he offers classes and tutorials for Jews of all ages and stages, and he lectures for shuls and school groups. His writing has been featured in a wide variety of publications, from *Binah* and *Inyan* magazines to the *Boston College Law Review*. Rabbi Viders circulates a popular weekly email enjoyed by all types of Jews. He can be reached at jmviders@gmail.com.

About
Mosaica
Press

Mosaica Press is an independent publisher of Jewish books. Our authors include some of the most profound, interesting, and entertaining thinkers and writers in the Jewish community today. Our books are available around the world. Please visit us at www.mosaicapress.com or contact us at info@mosaicapress.com. We will be glad to hear from you.